How to Manage Meetings

THE SUNDAY TIMES

How to Manage Meetings

Alan Barker | Second Edition

KoganPage

LONDON PHILADELPHIA NEW DELHI

Publisher's note

Every possible effort has been made to ensure that the information contained in this book is accurate at the time of going to press, and the publishers and author cannot accept responsibility for any errors or omissions, however caused. No responsibility for loss or damage occasioned to any person acting, or refraining from action, as a result of the material in this publication can be accepted by the editor, the publisher or the author.

First published in Great Britain and the United States in 2002 by Kogan Page Limited
Reprinted 2003, 2005
Second edition 2011

120 Pentonville Road	1518 Walnut Street, Suite 1100	4737/23 Ansari Road
London N1 9JN	Philadelphia PA 19102	Daryaganj
United Kingdom	USA	New Delhi 110002
www.koganpage.com		India

ISBN   978 0 7494 6342 7
E-ISBN   978 0 7494 6343 3

The views expressed in this book are those of the author, and are not necessarily the same as those of Times Newspapers Ltd.

British Library Cataloguing-in-Publication Data

A CIP record for this book is available from the British Library.

Library of Congress Cataloging-in-Publication Data

Barker, Alan, 1956–
    How to manage meetings / Alan Barker.
       p. cm.
    2nd ed. of: How to manage meetings, 2007.
    ISBN 978-0-7494-6342-7 -- ISBN 978-0-7494-6343-4 1. Business meetings. I. Title.
    HF5734.5.B37 2011
    658.4'56--dc22

                                                            2011002376

Typeset by Jean Cussons Typesetting, Diss, Norfolk
Printed and bound in India by Replika Press Pvt Ltd

Contents

Introduction

Meetings are indispensable when you don't want to do anything.

These words, by the great economist J K Galbraith, are now almost proverbial. Ask any manager to describe the meetings they attend: the words 'boring', 'worthless' and 'time-wasting' are almost guaranteed to crop up. The interminable meeting, at which people are surfing on their laptops or quietly dozing, is more or less a cliché of working life – endless fodder for *Dilbert* or *The Office*.

The cliché may have some grounding in truth. In a recent survey by Microsoft, 69 per cent of 38,000 respondents claimed that the meetings they attended were unproductive. Indeed, they listed ineffective meetings as among the top three time-wasters at work.

These complaints, however, may not tell the whole story. When Steven G Rogelberg and colleagues at the University of North Carolina probed more deeply, they found that people who complained publicly about meetings tended to feel rather differently about them in private: 59 per cent actually rated them as good to excellent, with only 15 per cent rating them poor or worse.

The relationship between meetings and job satisfaction is similarly nuanced. Rogelberg found that the people who most disliked the prospect of more meetings tended to be self-motivated and aggressively goal oriented; less obsessively single-minded managers actually liked the idea of meeting more. Perhaps they valued meetings for the social opportunities they offered or the discipline they brought to an otherwise vague work schedule.

It's not simply a case of 'Meetings, bloody meetings'. Video Arts' best-selling video may have contributed to the myth that most meetings are disastrous, but there is a danger of mistaking caricature for reality.

Why, then, has the image of the meeting from hell become so popular? I think it appeals to us not because so many meetings are so dreadful, but because we value meetings for what they can achieve, and we know that even the best meeting can be improved. Meetings matter.

And we shouldn't forget that meetings are costly. A two-hour meeting at middle-management level, including travel costs and opportunity costs, can easily become a four-figure investment, in whatever currency we choose. We *must* improve the way we manage meetings – and urgently.

This book will help you achieve that goal.

A meeting is a group of people thinking together. That's the governing idea of this book. Chapter 1 looks at what meetings are, why we hold them (and why we *should* hold them!), how meetings are changing and the golden rules that apply to every meeting. Chapter 2 explores the way groups behave. The complexities of group dynamics can be daunting, but if we can understand something of how groups operate, we'll be better prepared to participate as group members at our next meeting.

Groups think together, principally by holding conversations. Chapter 3 examines how conversations work, why they go wrong and how we can improve the conversations we hold in our meetings.

Managing the conversation in a meeting requires skill, as well as protocols and more or less formal rules. Using the drills well – the agenda, the minutes, the elements of procedural control – is obviously important. And we need to prepare these elements if they are to function properly. Chapter 4 contains all you need to know to prepare for a meeting.

Leading a meeting is a key managerial skill. Meetings are where managers are most clearly visible as managers, and where leaders can be seen to lead. Chairing a meeting gives us the opportunity to make a real impact: on our team, our colleagues, our customers and our own managers. Chapter 5 concentrates on the responsibilities of chairing.

The Chair's main role should be to help the group think more effectively together. Most of us have had little formal training in thinking. Chapter 6 brings together the material on conversation and on groups to explore how we can improve the way groups can think more effectively: how we can build some simple discipline into the conversations we hold, and how we can record that thinking visually.

Chapter 7 looks at the varied skills we all need to improve the way we participate in meetings. To participate – fully and positively – means more than making your voice heard and getting your point across. It means taking a full part in the group conversation: helping others to make their points well, encouraging and guiding, listening and responding appropriately.

Most meetings involve solving problems of some kind. Chapter 8 looks at problem-solving. The format of the meeting may vary according to the kind of problem we are tackling.

Chapter 9 is a reminder of what needs to happen *after* a meeting to ensure that it has effective outcomes and has not been a waste of time.

We meet for all sorts of reasons and, increasingly, in different ways. Chapter 10 explores various formats of meeting, including team meetings and negotiation. It also considers the challenges to meetings from new technologies and new modes of working:

how to navigate the perils of international meetings, conference calls, videoconferencing and web meetings.

We're all responsible for the success of the meetings we attend. Whether as a Chair, a participant or a minute-taker, we can all find ways to manage meetings better. If you are frustrated at the waste of time, effort and energy in your organisation's meetings – and if you want to do something about it – then this book is for you.

Numerous people have offered me their thoughts as I prepared this new edition. Some I know only through their published work; I acknowledge them in Chapter 11. Others I have met in person or online; some are trusted colleagues. In particular, I am grateful (in alphabetical order) to Angelique Bakker, Paul Boniface, Jenny Davenport, Robin Davies (who introduced me to Tudor Rickards' work and the powerful idea of a 'How to' session), Simon Drury, Tim Fearon, Tom Flatau (who drew my attention to rich pictures), Eric Galvin, a blogger I know only as 'Grant', Janis Grummitt, Malcolm Holt, Uta Langley, John McDermott, Simon Meijlink, Glenn Parker, Megan Roberts, Alex Sherman, Duncan Smith of Mindlab International, Phil Sproston, Val Tyler, Berry Winter and Steve Young. They have all inspired me; any inadequacies in the finished book, of course, are entirely mine.

1

What is a meeting?

Meetings are at the very heart of management. A recent survey suggested that 11 million meetings are held in the United States each day. That might translate to about 2.2 million business meetings in the UK every day, or about 40,000 meetings daily per million of population in any developed country. Other research suggests that most employees spend about six hours a week in meetings, and that the amount of time increases as we climb the organisational ladder. Senior managers may attend as much as 23 hours of meetings in a week. People in large organisations tend to have more meetings than workers in small enterprises.

Meetings have two important dimensions, related to task and to social relationships. On the one hand, meetings help us to move our business forward. It's in meetings that we share ideas and brainstorm new ones; that we evaluate options and develop the best of them into feasible solutions. On the other hand, we shouldn't ignore the social dimension. It's in meetings that we can be *seen* to make our contribution. Meetings allow us to hold real conversations; they allow us to articulate our vision to others and to collaborate; and they provide a mechanism for building social relationships and networks. Meetings articulate an organisation's culture.

And meetings can take many forms. That encounter by the water cooler might produce results just as valuable as any formally convened meeting around a board table. Some organisations actively encourage huddles in the corridor: everybody standing, no coffee or biscuits. And increasingly, meetings are now happening online, using tools like Skype or GoToMeeting.

What connects all these different events? What makes a meeting a meeting?

A group thinking together

Here, for starters, is a brief definition:

A meeting is a group of people thinking purposefully together.

This simple definition distinguishes meetings from interviews – where the conversation is led by one person and focused on another – and from casual chats in the pub or the company restaurant. Let's briefly examine the two key elements of this definition.

First, a meeting involves *a group of people*. To be sure, we attend meetings as individuals, but we also behave as members of a group. What we do in a meeting will be affected by our relationship to the group: whether we feel comfortable or ill at ease, whether we feel a sense of belonging or alienation, whether we feel in control or at the mercy of others' private agendas. And the group in any meeting also has its own behaviour, governed by the principles of group dynamics. To ignore the behaviour of the group *as a group* is to risk mismanaging the meeting.

Secondly, the group is *thinking together*. This doesn't mean that we are thinking the same thing. Far from it. The Chair has called us together because we have diverse views, experiences and expertise. People should be voicing different opinions; why else hold the conversation? But the group also needs discipline in the meeting. We should be thinking together: we should know the reason for meeting, the kind of thinking we should be doing at any point, and what we hope to achieve. And we each have a responsibility to help the group think together.

Why hold meetings?

The final part of our definition includes that word 'purposefully'. A meeting is a conversation with objectives. How many meetings are held out of habit or with no clear sense of purpose? Too often, we walk away from a meeting wondering why we met.

If we want to improve the quality of our meetings, we must start with a better sense of why we want to hold meetings at all. Establishing a clear reason for meeting is the first step towards success.

So what's the best reason for holding a meeting? The simple answer is: 'when the task requires a group of people to think about it.' If the task does not need a group of people to complete it, then a meeting should be unnecessary.

The most obvious task that *doesn't* need a group to complete it is the delivery of information. Those briefings in which senior managers gather the staff together to announce the latest decree – or in which middle managers are called up to 'cascade' information from senior levels downwards – are among the most ineffective meetings. Information presented in this way is likely to be misinterpreted or forgotten.

There is some evidence that 'team briefings' of this kind are on the wane. 'People are *finally* starting to realise', says John McDermott, a consultant based in Santa Fe, 'that meetings are not the best tool for one-way info dissemination. Unless there is the need or desire for interaction, a meeting can often be replaced by a memo, video or intranet document posting.'

Here are some powerful reasons for holding meetings:

- *To exchange and evaluate information.* Meetings help us understand what others in the team are doing, and how that fits with our own work. Meetings help us to avoid duplicating tasks and locate our work in a larger context. In meetings, we can see the bigger picture.

  A group can evaluate information more effectively than a single person. In groups, we can bring multiple perspectives to bear on information, resulting in fewer gross errors of understanding. Gathering, exchanging and evaluating information are important activities in any organisation.

  Briefings exchange and evaluate information in a particular way. Staff survey consultations, or meetings between consultants and clients, all have this aim. Team leaders explain higher-level decisions and changes so that the team can see how they are affected. In exchange, the team can check their understanding, evaluate how the changes will affect their work and build their commitment to them. Critically, team briefings also allow the team to send their responses to change – and their own ideas – back 'up the line'.
- *To solve problems.* Virtually all meetings will involve problem-solving of some kind. A group's success in solving a problem depends on the quality of its thinking: not only how much thinking it does, but also *how* it thinks.

  Problems tend to fit into two very broad categories: situations that are unsatisfactory in some way, or challenges arising from a change in circumstances. We need to be able to define the problem well and choose the thinking tools that will best help us solve it.

  Groups are not good at solving problems that need expert knowledge or subtle reasoning. With such problems, the group will only think as well as its most competent member.

- *To resolve conflict*. Meetings can help to find the source of conflict and to explore different ways of dealing with it. The most obvious example of such a meeting would be a negotiation (though not all negotiations start from a position of conflict, of course).

    Conflict can easily arise within any kind of meeting. Solving problems and evaluating information can cause arguments that the group must resolve if its thinking is to move forward. Building or repairing morale at times of change and uncertainty can often mean resolving conflicts.
- *To inspire*. Humans are biologically gregarious. Very few of us can get through a day comfortably without interacting with others. We *like* to meet, especially if our work tends to be solitary. Meetings give meaning to our work by relating it to the work of others; they can help us through difficulties by allowing us to share problems. The support of the group energises and motivates individuals to perform better. Group members who set their own goals often demand more of themselves than their superiors do.

Meetings are natural events. They appeal to deep-seated needs for social contact and a sense of belonging. We can emerge from a successful meeting energised, committed and enthusiastic. In contrast, the damage done by poor meetings is probably far greater than we realise. A poorly managed meeting may cause more harm – in terms of frustration, confusion and poor morale – than a meeting that is cancelled.

Why meetings fail

There is usually no mystery about why meetings fail. We can identify a small number of factors that are at the heart of poor meetings management:

- *The meeting is unnecessary*. The job could be done in some simpler, cheaper way: it is routine and does not need to be discussed; the information can be exchanged on paper or electronically. Perhaps only one or two people need to be involved, or the problem needs the attention of a single expert. Perhaps there is nothing to be done at all!
- *The meeting is held for the wrong reason*. To discuss, to decree or to demolish: all common reasons for holding meetings, and all inadequate. Managers often call meetings merely to wield power over others, or to pursue some private agenda. They use the meeting to rubberstamp or steamroller decisions.

  Many meetings happen as a matter of habit: a habit that nobody dares challenge. They can be primarily social occasions: a chance to 'get away from the desk'. Meetings of this kind are group therapy in disguise: they are held to avoid loneliness.
- *The objective of the meeting is unclear*. Nobody has asked why the meeting is being held. Nobody knows its purpose; people have not received or read any of the supporting papers. The agenda is vague and unhelpful, or does not exist.
- *The wrong people are there*. Or the right people are absent. Do you need to be involved in this conversation? Are the decision-makers here? Sometimes nobody at the meeting has the authority to decide what to do. Sometimes substitutes are sent at the last minute, who are ill informed and unable to take responsibility.
- *Lack of proper control*. The procedure of the meeting is unclear; timekeeping is appalling; the discussion rambles from point to point; hidden agendas hijack the proceedings; conflict, when it occurs, is not properly managed. Blame for any or all of these problems is usually laid at the feet of a weak Chair, but a dictatorial Chair who represses discussion rather than controlling it can be just as damaging.

- *Poor environment*. The venue is inappropriate or uncomfortable; facilities are poor; disruptions destroy concentration.
- *Poor timing*. It is the wrong time of day/week/month/year to make the decision; the meeting fails to start or end on time; people arrive late or leave early.

Meetings will not improve by magic. They must be managed. You must want change – and be willing to implement it. You must also know the tools and techniques that will help you improve the quality of the meetings you attend – as the Chair, as a participant or as the administrator.

Improving the way a group of people thinks can be difficult. Sometimes only a policy decision will do the trick. Even if your organisation does not implement systematic change, you can change your own behaviour. If you hold – or attend – meetings, you have an opportunity to improve them. The longest journey starts with a single step: and somebody has to take it. Why not you?

How meetings are changing

Meetings are evolving. Three factors, in particular, seem to be influencing the way meetings will look in the future.

More and more meetings

All the signs are that we are meeting more than we used to. One study suggests that executive meetings doubled in number between the 1960s and the 1980s. In a more recent study, 72 per cent of 1,900 business leaders reported spending more time in meetings than they had done five years previously; almost half of them expected time in meetings to increase still further.

Why these increases? To begin with, work is simply more complicated than it used to be. Organisational structures have changed: flatter hierarchies, outsourcing and networking all demand more active collaboration. Many of our meetings are now with people we may not know well: project team members, clients or suppliers, consultants and contractors. We need to be able to work together quickly, with minimal introductions. In addition, managers increasingly feel that employees have important information and ideas, and that they should involve people, consult them and empower them. Meetings are the obvious way to do all of these things.

The rise of teamwork has also created the need for more meetings. Teams are high-maintenance: they need to meet regularly to maintain their identity, to understand what they have to do and to help them find their place in the wider organisation. The natural communication tool of the team is the meeting. As the number of teams increases, so the number of meetings goes up.

Not only are organisations more team-based, but they are becoming global. 'The challenge', suggests Glenn Parker, a team-building consultant based in New Jersey, 'is how to plan and manage groups of people who speak many different languages, represent a variety of cultures and who must invariably meet via teleconference or videoconference.'

Technology

In the face of such developments, and the soaring costs of travel, managers are increasingly turning to technology to meet more efficiently.

The most obvious technological change in business meetings has been the rise of the remote meeting. Telephone conferencing has been around for some decades. According to Malcolm Holt of the Telephone Museum in Milton Keynes, UK:

The introduction of the loud-speaking telephone in 1959 enabled a small group to speak to others for the first time. The 'telephone' was in the form of a small desk console with a microphone and loudspeaker; it was voice-switched: only one end could speak at a time; any interruption would cut out the other speaker's voice. Very good for discipline at meetings!

Videoconferencing appeared in 1971, with the advent of a product called Confravision. Pictures (in black and white) were transmitted over microwave links between dedicated studios in London, Birmingham, Manchester, Glasgow and Bristol. Half a dozen people – plus a secretary – could be in view in each studio. The service was expensive: £120 per hour (about half the average weekly wage at the time). Videoconferencing evolved slowly over the next 20 years, and then took a leap forward with the advent of the internet. Cheap webcams and web-based tools like Skype have slashed the cost of videoconferencing.

Other tools have had less obvious effects on meetings management. Groupware like Microsoft Exchange (also known as Outlook Calendar) allows everyone to see everyone's diaries, making arranging a meeting relatively effortless. The result – particularly in project-based organisations and the IT industry – has been an explosion of meetings. To quote an anonymous blogger who writes as 'Grant':

> I can now, in five minutes, take an hour of time from 10 people by scheduling a meeting with them. Since I can see their calendars, they're even robbed of most convenient excuses. What's more, I can now easily schedule meetings with numbers of people that would have been quite impractical the old way.

What was advertised as a solution has become a problem: more meetings, with larger groups, less well prepared.

But technology is beginning to do more than clog our diaries with more meetings or create the sophisticated illusion of a real meeting room. The very definition of a meeting seems to be changing. New tools are creating new forms of conversation.

Megan Roberts, a research consultant at Oxford Innovation, is a typical early adopter of these new technologies. 'You can collaborate on work before you get to the point of having a meeting,' she says, 'with tools like wikis, Huddle and other collaborative software.' The conversation that once was held in one place at one time, now takes place as an exchange of messages in cyberspace. There is evidence, also, that younger people are increasingly using social networking sites as ways of holding conversations.

Reactions to all this new technology seem to vary, unsurprisingly, between the generations. Jenny Davenport of People in Business, a London-based consultancy, cites research suggesting that older people see conference calls as a necessary evil or as a second-best substitute for a meeting, while younger people seem them as a welcome opportunity to multitask.

More haste, less courtesy

Multitasking is just one aspect of a change in meeting etiquette. The increasing pace of work is another. As decisions become more last-minute and working patterns become more complex, meetings seem to be happening with less advance notice and less preparation. Meetings are becoming shorter, as managers try to shave costs (in itself, surely no bad thing). Participants may have to travel further at shorter notice to avoid accommodation costs. They may find less in the way of refreshments on the table when they arrive.

Meetings are becoming less formal – perhaps less well organised. 'Meetings are becoming less structured', says Val Tyler, a UK-based management consultant. 'Agendas tend to be written and updated at the last minute. Minutes – if they exist – will be written up and circulated fast. I see more and more paperless meetings, in which the agenda is not written down.'

The increasing pace of work has consequences for meeting etiquette too. People arrive late and leave early; they expect to have their mobile phones on – and may even take calls – during the meeting. They manage their e-mails on their smartphones or surf on their laptops. Older people might call this behaviour simple rudeness; younger folk welcome it as 'multitasking'.

The three golden rules of effective meetings

This book is about how to manage meetings for everybody's benefit. Every idea and technique here is based on three golden rules:

- *Schedule only necessary meetings.* **Why hold a meeting? Because you are looking for some specific output that you can achieve only by means of a group of people thinking together. Eliminate update or status meetings, where the only objective is to disseminate information. If there is no identifiable reason for holding the meeting, or if those objectives can be achieved in other ways, ask yourself whether the meeting is necessary.**

   This is particularly so with regular meetings: weekly team meetings, project meetings or committee meetings. The agenda for every meeting must be unique. Meetings are too expensive to hold for no good reason.
- *Make everybody responsible for the meeting's success.* **Obviously, the Chair bears the primary responsibility for how the meeting is conducted. But each participant should have a role to play. Invite only those people who need to be involved in the issue. Idle people at a meeting are pure cost.**

   Don't forget your minute-taker. They, too, can take on some core responsibilities in the meeting: keeping time, summarising, collating action points and, of

course, completing an accurate record of the meeting's progress and outcomes.

- *Check the action points that result from your meeting.* Make a habit of writing an action list after every meeting you hold. What will happen after it finishes? Could you have agreed and delegated any of those actions without holding the meeting? Is responsibility for them allocated clearly to named individuals? Do they have exact deadlines? Who will monitor progress?

    If all we do at the end of a meeting is arrange another meeting, something has gone seriously wrong.

A meeting is a group of people thinking purposefully together. The principal way we think together is by holding a conversation. In the next chapter, then, we shall look at groups: at how they work and how we can help them to operate more effectively in meetings. Chapter 3 looks at the central tool of meetings: the conversation.

2

How groups work

A meeting is a group in action. To manage meetings more effectively, we need to know something about how groups behave: what they are, how they develop, the structures that emerge from that development, and how those structures encourage or discourage certain kinds of behaviour in our meetings.

We can define a group as any number of people who interact with each other in some way, are aware of each other and perceive themselves to be a group. A viable group, by our definition, has about 12 members (about the maximum size of a sports team). Any larger meeting will become hard to manage, and sub-groups will emerge. Hence the need for rigorous procedures at annual general meetings and other large meetings.

Groups have two kinds of objectives. Task objectives may be imposed or dictated from outside the group: by the agenda, or by the Chair. Social objectives concern the group's developing sense of identity, its well-being and the relationships within it. They usually develop from within the group.

Groups can be formal or informal. The more formal the group, the more task oriented it will be; the more informal, the more socially oriented. Formal groups – committees or company boards – are created to accomplish particular tasks. Informal groups emerge spontaneously as we associate with each other, exchanging experiences and enjoying each other's company. Both kinds of group exist in organisations. Informal groups, broadly speaking, satisfy the human needs that formal groups neglect or ignore.

A group in a meeting will probably be pursuing both task and social objectives. We know that people value meetings as much for their social value as for the opportunities they offer to make a work contribution. We need to manage both task and social objectives. We should clarify task objectives: identifying our goals, expressing them clearly on an agenda, keeping the meeting focused on results. But we ignore social objectives at our peril.

Individuals and groups

Groups affect individuals' behaviour. In turn, we can influence the groups we join. When we join a group, we want to fit in. As individuals, we pursue the essential aims of:

- **well-being (physical, mental, emotional, economic, spiritual);**
- **a sense of belonging;**
- **recognition from the group;**
- **control over our own lives.**

If the group satisfies these needs, we will respond by strengthening it. If a meeting satisfies – or at least addresses – these needs in the participants, then they will be prepared to contribute more fully to it.

How groups develop

The group itself, meanwhile, begins to take on a life of its own. It wants, above all, to survive. And it will develop in pursuit of that aim.

Perhaps the most highly influential model of group development was created by Barry Tuckman in the 1960s. As with so much organisational research, Tuckman's began in a military context. After completing his doctorate at Princeton, Tuckman worked for the US Navy, studying small group behaviour. His manager asked him to organise and integrate 50 studies of group development. Tuckman looked for a developmental sequence that would fit most of the studies. In his own words:

> I hit on four stages going from (1) orientation/testing/dependence, to (2) conflict, to (3) group cohesion, to (4) functional role-relatedness. For these I coined the terms: 'forming,' 'storming,' 'norming,' and 'performing.'

We can apply Tuckman's model to meetings and derive some useful strategies for managing them.

Forming

At the first stage, relationships are tentative. We're finding out about each other: our attitudes, background and values. We are also keen to establish our own identities and make an impression. We may be anxious or embarrassed.

Forming: key behaviours

- **Individuals orientate themselves in relation to the group – primarily through testing.**
- **Testing identifies boundaries of interpersonal and task behaviours.**

- **Individuals establish dependency relationships with the leader and other group members, or with pre-existing standards, rules or conventions.**

In a meeting, the Chair should bring the group safely through this period of uncertainty. They must strengthen the group quickly, by identifying what binds it together and by stating the rules governing its behaviour. They should define tasks and allocate responsibilities clearly.

Forming: Chair's key role

- *Overview*. Setting objectives and rules.
- *Direction*. High.
- *Support*. Low.
- *Key focus*. Individual tasks.
- *Persuasion style*. Tell/push.
- *Team interaction*. Leader provides links.

Storming

The second stage is characterised by conflict. Group members challenge each other's versions of reality: where we agree and where we differ. At a dinner party, this is the 'politics and religion' stage, and can be uncomfortable; in a meeting, versions of reality may be disguised in terms of action: preferred methods of working.

The group will be at its most vulnerable at the storming stage. Power politics can come into play. Relationships established in the forming stage might be disrupted or destroyed. Individuals will try tactical manoeuvres: seeking allies, withdrawing ('wait and see'), empire building or hijacking the proceedings.

For some groups, the pressure of storming can become too great: the meeting breaks down (formal negotiations can end like this). Some groups never move beyond the storming stage, and formalise conflict into a regular procedure (political committees, for example, often become stuck in permanent storming).

Members of the group may try to resolve conflict by agreeing a version of reality: the value and belief systems to which everybody can 'sign up'.

Storming: key behaviours

- **Conflict occurs.**
- **Individuals polarise around interpersonal issues.**
- **There are emotional responses to task behaviours.**
- **There is resistance to group influence and task requirements.**

The Chair has a critical role to play. By recognising and acknowledging diverse views, they can help the group to understand tasks more deeply, as well as strengthening social relationships by celebrating the value of different perspectives. Conflict is potentially creative, and if the group can survive conflict it has demonstrated some core values that will serve it well in the future.

Storming: Chair's key role

- *Overview*. Resolve conflicts.
- *Direction*. High.
- *Support*. High.
- *Key focus*. People interactions.
- *Persuasion style*. Sell/consult.
- *Team interaction*. Facilitate relationships.

Norming

The group has found a shared frame of reference: an agreed version of reality based on common perceptions, values and beliefs. These are the group's norms. It now develops a way of working to achieve its goals, allocating roles and rules of conduct: a practical framework in which people can work together.

During the norming stage, 'groupthink' can emerge. The term was apparently coined by the analyst and journalist William H Whyte in 1952. Whyte defined the term as 'a rationalised conformity – an open, articulate philosophy that holds that group values are not only expedient but right and good as well'. Anybody who refuses to accept the norms may be labelled as 'deviant' or 'subversive'. (There's more about groupthink, and about Irving Janis, who made the term famous, in Chapter 5.)

Norming: key behaviours

- The group overcomes resistance by developing in-group feelings and cohesiveness.
- New standards (norms) evolve for group and task behaviours.
- Individuals adopt new roles.
- Intimate personal opinions are expressed in relation to the task.

The Chair of a group that has successfully reached the norming stage can afford to become less directive and more facilitative. By concentrating on the process of the group's thinking, they can give the group more room to do its own work. But they may also need to challenge 'groupthink' by reminding the group of how things are in the world outside the meeting room. They may need to challenge the group with new ideas.

Norming: Chair's key role

- *Overview.* Facilitate processes.
- *Direction.* Low.
- *Support.* High.
- *Key focus.* Task interactions.
- *Persuasion style.* Listen/advise.
- *Team interaction.* Facilitate team processes.

Performing

The group gets on with the job in hand. It's fully mature, clearly understands the task, and adapts its behaviour to achieve it. Roles within the group are flexible, and norms include the acceptance of diverse opinions and change. The group understands the context of its work and looks outward beyond its own concerns.

Performing: key behaviours

- **Interpersonal structure becomes the tool of task activities.**
- **Roles become flexible and functional.**
- **Group energy is channelled to the task.**
- **Structural issues have been resolved.**
- **Structure now supports task performance.**

The Chair blessed with such a group in a meeting can lead with the lightest of touches. Directional behaviour and resolving conflict gives way to observing, supporting and coaching.

Performing: Chair's key role

- *Overview.* Coach.
- *Direction.* Low.
- *Support.* Low.
- *Key focus.* Team self-development.
- *Persuasion style.* Observe/support.
- *Team interaction.* Dynamic grouping.

How accurate is Tuckman's model? And how useful is it in the context of meetings?

First, group development can occur on different timescales. One group could go through all four stages in a couple of hours (and some meetings could witness that complete development); others grow into maturity over months (and will display the characteristics of one stage in a meeting).

Secondly, groups don't always develop in the neat linear manner suggested by Tuckman's model. Some groups become stuck in an early stage – sometimes irretrievably. If group members are seeking to balance the demands of a task with the demands of group cohesion, the group may alternate between two stages: typically, between storming and norming. A group may switch to a new mode as members leave and new members arrive.

Neither of these qualifications negates the value of Tuckman's model. Rather, they indicate that, with care, the model can provide powerful clues about what's going on in a meeting. In particular, it can help us:

- **appreciate why conversations in groups differ from conversations between individuals;**
- **anticipate conflict and prevent or tackle it;**
- **manage the group's behaviour;**
- **improve the output or results of the meeting.**

Understanding the structure of groups

As the group evolves through these four stages, it develops a structure. We seek predictability in a group: uncertainty about others' behaviour can threaten a group's sense of identity. The group's structure provides a 'system of solutions' to the threat of unpredictable behaviour.

Group structure is neither fixed nor permanent. A group is a complex, dynamic system, operating along a number of dimensions, including:

- **status;**
- **power;**
- **role;**
- **leadership;**
- **liking.**

We can interpret people's behaviour in a meeting as evidence of their efforts to find their place in the group structure, to move within it or to challenge it.

Status

Each position in the group has a value assigned to it. That status may be formal or social. Formal status comprises the collection of rights and duties associated with a position. Social status is the rank of a person as measured by the group: the degree of respect, familiarity or reserve the group gives to that person.

Our status in a group is always at risk. A group confers status on anybody who meets the group's expectations. We create our status entirely through others' perceptions (we may call it 'good name' or 'reputation'). It can be destroyed or diminished in a moment. Downgrading a person's status in the group can be a powerful way of exerting the group's authority.

Power

We could define power as the control we can exert over others. John French and Bertram Raven, in the late 1950s, identified five kinds of power:

- *Reward power*. The ability to grant favours for behaviour.
- *Coercive power*. The ability to punish others.
- *Legitimate power*. Conferred by law or other sets of rules.
- *Referent power*. The 'charisma' that causes others to imitate or idolise.
- *Expert power*. Deriving from specific levels of knowledge or skill.

People may seek to exercise different kinds of power at different times. A participant in a meeting who has little reward power may seize an opportunity to influence the meeting as an expert; a Chair who lacks charisma or respect may try to exert authority by appealing to legitimate or even coercive power.

A group can exercise power of its own. Norms – the accepted rules of engagement within the group, and the agreed view of reality that members of the group share – are the means by which the group wields power. To violate these norms threatens the very identity of the group. Groups will, therefore, often put pressure on people to conform. Their members may be:

- encouraged: by humour, gentle sarcasm, pointed remarks;
- embarrassed: categorised as weak, stupid, irresponsible, odd – even evil;
- excluded: temporarily but deliberately left out of the conversation; or
- expelled: told to 'shut up or get out'.

As participants, we can respond to this pressure in one of three ways. We can:

- **argue our case, fight our corner and try to persuade others to join us;**
- **conform and suppress any opinion or behaviour that offends the group; or**
- **withdraw.**

What we do will depend on our location in the group structure. If we have a great deal of power, we may easily persuade the group to change its norms in our favour. If we have high status or are much liked, the group may tolerate deviant behaviour rather than lose a valuable member.

Role

Our role in the meeting affects the set of behaviours the group expects of us. We can think of roles in terms of task and social function.

Task roles have been explored extensively; Meredith Belbin's are probably the most famous. Thousands of managers have now used Belbin's questionnaire to locate themselves among his categories of:

- **Chair/co-ordinator;**
- **shaper/team leader;**
- **plant/innovator or creative thinker;**
- **monitor-evaluator/critical thinker;**
- **company worker/implementer;**
- **teamworker/team builder;**
- **finisher/detail checker and pusher;**
- **resource investigator/researcher outside the team.**

Recently, Belbin has felt the need to add a further role, that of expert. A successful team will contain a balance of all nine roles; a team too strong in any one or more will perform less successfully. The same may be said to be true of meetings, though our ability to improve the balance by changing the group may be limited.

Leadership

This dimension of group structure is closely related to all the others, even if a leader is imposed on the group from outside.

We can define leadership as behaviour that helps the group to achieve its preferred objectives. Research in the 1950s distinguished between autocratic, democratic and laissez-faire styles of leadership and their respective effects on the performance of groups. The concept of leadership itself has changed radically since then, as command-and-control structures in organisations have given way – at least to some extent – to flatter structures. Leadership is now often referred to as a 'facilitative' activity: doing whatever allows the group to achieve, rather than directing people's energy in a certain direction.

It's useful, particularly in the context of meetings, to distinguish between task leadership and process leadership. The first focuses on the job to be done, the second on building good relations within the group.

Liking

The liking dimension emerges spontaneously, helping to gain people status or power, or allowing them to exercise effective leadership.

The distinction between liking and disliking seems simplistic. We can find others attractive in many different ways or take against them in ways we may not be able – or willing – to articulate. Liking can become an emotional entanglement or even a fully-fledged relationship; dislike can turn into a vendetta or a curious, half-coded game of tit for tat. We may be unaware of the structures of like and dislike in the group at a meeting, and may have to rely on clues.

How groups behave

Broadly, we can divide behaviour in meetings into:

- **task behaviour: contributions to the meeting's work;**
- **process behaviour: helping the group to develop.**

A third category, non-functional behaviour, includes anything that hinders or prevents the meeting from succeeding in either its task or process objectives.

Distinguishing between these three categories can be difficult, especially if the meeting includes people of different cultural backgrounds. As the Chair of a meeting, focusing on objectives and targets – as well as the clock – you will be hard pressed to identify more than a few of these behaviours. You may be reacting to many of them unconsciously.

Task behaviours

- **initiating: defining a problem, redefining it, making suggestions, presenting new information, proposing solutions;**
- **seeking information;**
- **giving information;**
- **building and elaborating: developing ideas, giving examples, adding detail, creating scenarios;**
- **summarising: restating, reorganising information, repeating, clarifying;**
- **evaluating: for value or relevance;**
- **testing for consensus or disagreement.**

Process behaviours

- **encouraging: responding positively, praising, accepting;**
- **gate-keeping: letting others contribute;**
- **stopping: ending a line of argument that seems unproductive or counter-intuitive;**

- redirecting: from one person to another;
- mediating: in moments of conflict.

Non-functional behaviours
- aggression;
- self-confessing or sympathy seeking;
- seeking attention;
- negative or offensive humour;
- withdrawing.

Separating task direction from process direction can be useful. You may be able to use video or, better still, an external meetings auditor, to help you. However, picking and responding to only a few of these behaviours, then encouraging or discouraging them, can improve the group's performance substantially.

Managing the group

How then can we manage a group? It all seems so complicated! Managing people as individuals can be hard enough; managing groups of people looks well nigh impossible. Where can we start?

The first lesson is perhaps the hardest. If we don't manage the group, the group will manage itself. Whether we are chairing or participating, we will not manage the group successfully unless we work *with* it, rather than *against* it.

Here are some simple questions to set you thinking:

- *Can you see the group in this meeting as a group?* Or are they individuals who have little relationship to each other?
- *Are there obvious sub-groups within the group?* When a client group meets a supplier or provider group, for example, links within the sub-groups will be stronger

than between the two groups – at least to start with. The same will be true of meetings between management and union, or between different departments in a large organisation.

- *Can you clearly identify task and social objectives for the group?* Both need to be clear. Announce task objectives at the start of the meeting. It might also be worth building in a short 'social' period in which people can get to know each other, swap gossip or 'network'. The group's ability to think and work well depends as much on the relationships within the group as on clear task definition.
- *Can you identify any individual needs that may interfere with the objectives of the meeting?* Most 'people issues' in meetings can be traced back to an individual need that the group isn't fulfilling, for some reason. Some such issues can become chronic problems. Can you at least be forewarned of them? Perhaps you can take action to address that need within the meeting itself.
- *How far has the group developed?* Where are we in the Tuckman cycle? There are specific actions a Chair can take to guide a group through each stage. Participants can also help the group move from one stage to the next.
- *How can you influence the group's structure?* You may be able to identify where status or power are influential in the group. You may see people with high status or power as a threat to the group's well-being – or to your own authority as Chair. Perhaps you want to weaken such influences or undermine them. It might be better to work with these influences than against them. Give a powerful individual a challenging task; use status to build a team of co-workers within a project.

If you can identify some roles in the meeting, you may be able to exploit them. Draw on the creativity of your 'plants', or the thoroughness of the 'shapers' and 'finishers'. Use the diplomatic skills of the 'teamworkers' to weld the group together.

- *What behaviours do you want to encourage in the group?* **Think of the range of task and process behaviours in the group as a repertoire of behaviours that you can encourage and 'play', through your management of the conversation. Challenge non-functional behaviours rather than letting them take control.**

If a meeting is a group thinking together, then conversation is the means by which it thinks together. As well as understanding something about groups, managing a meeting means managing group conversations. That's what we'll look at next.

3

Conversation: the heart of the meeting

A meeting is a conversation. It's by conversing that we express our thinking and relationships to each other. If we want to improve our meetings, we must improve the quality of the conversations that take place in them.

What is conversation?

Conversation is a dynamic of talking and listening. These two activities do not happen merely in sequence, but simultaneously: each participant in a conversation both speaks and listens *throughout the conversation*. Our effectiveness in a conversation depends both on how well we talk, and on how well we listen.

We can think of conversation as a verbal dance. The word, from Latin, has the root meaning of 'to keep turning with'. Conversation relies for its success on moving together comfortably, without treading on each other's toes.

Like any dance, conversation has rules and standard moves. The most basic of these rules are rarely written down; most of us learn them experientially. Consequently, the rules vary subtly between cultures. Most cultures, however, will recognise these core rules of conversation (gathered together by Max Atkinson in his book *Lend Me Your Ears*):

- *One at a time*. Conversation involves turn-taking. If the other person interrupts us while we are speaking, it's natural to feel annoyed. Regular or habitual interruptions will have a catastrophic effect on our conversational reputation.
- *Come in on cue*. Imagine saying 'Good morning' to someone – and they don't reply at all. You know that they have good hearing, and that they speak your language. Perhaps they are cutting you dead. Perhaps you've offended them.

  Plainly, none of us would want to create such negative thoughts in another person (well, most of the time!). So, as well as obeying the rule of turn-taking, we must come in on cue, after the other person has finished speaking but before the silence has become uncomfortable. (This period of acceptable silence between turns in a conversation differs across cultures.)
- *Show that you are listening*. We are very sensitive to any signs that someone isn't listening to us. Giving eye contact to the speaker, and using 'minimal encouragers' – grunts, nods, little 'uh-huh's, and so on – are important cues to the other person that we are paying attention.
- *Be ready to say something relevant*. When we take our turn in the conversation, we need to say something that directly relates to what the speaker has just said. If we want to avoid or change the subject, we may need to say so explicitly: 'If you don't mind, I'd rather not talk about that', or 'Just to change the subject for a moment...'

These basic rules compel us to pay attention in a conversation. We need to avoid interrupting, to come in on cue, to show that we are listening and to say something relevant, and these constant demands are all powerful incentives to stay awake and alert.

Why conversations go wrong in meetings

How many of the meetings we attend are involving, open, comfortable and successful? Some, no doubt, are all of these things, but many are not. And it seems that the very nature of a business meeting can be inimical to good conversation, because a meeting's structure can violate the basic rules we've just examined.

Lack of involvement

The dynamics of conversation change subtly as the number of people involved increases. These changes in dynamic can easily come into conflict with the protocols we associate with meetings.

For example, a conversation between two people is – or should be – absorbing, or even intense. With three people, that intensity relaxes: whoever isn't speaking can choose whether to compete to speak next, or to opt out and let the other person speak. With four people, two simultaneous conversations become possible, although having a one-in-three chance of speaking next still gives each person a reasonable opportunity to remain involved in a single conversation.

With seven people or more, that chance of speaking next in a single conversation has diminished significantly. Given the choice, people will choose to hold a conversation with only one or two others, and multiple conversations will emerge. The resulting 'buzz' of noise gives an impression of liveliness and fellowship: a good time is had by all.

The critical number – what Atkinson calls 'the point of

maximum tension' – is five (or perhaps six). With a group of this size, each participant will ask: is this a single conversation, giving me a one-in-five chance of speaking? Or can I set up a separate conversation with the person next to me?

We can now see that meetings can easily violate the natural dynamics of conversation. They are often held with groups of five or more. If the cardinal rule is that only one conversation happens at a time, most people in the group will feel – for most of the time – that the four basic rules of conversation don't apply to them: there is no need to show that they are listening, come in on cue or say anything relevant! And no need to speak one at a time. Most importantly, no need to pay attention.

If people say that they don't feel involved in meetings, one reason may be that the meeting violates the basic rules of conversation. Why should we feel involved in a non-conversation?

Lack of openness

Meetings are notoriously prone to politics. Anything we say is more or less public, and we can be held accountable for it. Along with all the complex group dynamics that may be at play, it's no wonder that what's said in a meeting sometimes bears only a vague relationship to what we really think.

Lack of ease

It's not surprising, then, that meetings can be uncomfortable events. The more or less unnatural quality of conversation in a meeting, together with the politics that may be lurking below the surface, can contribute to a distinct sense of unease.

Some managers are looking for ways to combat this sense of unease. Simon Drury, who runs The Motivation Continuum, welcomes anything that re-energises people: 'There's nothing like having a quick and dirty meeting "off campus", for a different energy and perspective,' he says, 'in the park, a local hotel lobby, or Starbucks.' Uta Langley is another consultant who sees the rules of formality disappearing. 'Huddles in the corridor or office are popular with my clients at the moment,' she says. 'Everybody stands up, it's quick and short – and there's no coffee or biscuits.'

Interestingly, young people seem to feel this sense of unease more strongly than older ones. Perhaps they are simply less hardened to it. Jenny Davenport suggests that younger people may find meetings genuinely harder to handle. 'For the baby-boomers and Generation X-ers,' she says, 'who were born between about 1950 and 1980, meetings feel like a vital way to communicate. For Generation Y, who are currently in their twenties and early thirties, meetings can seem uncomfortable, confrontational and overly formal.'

Lack of success

And so back to the core complaint: that meetings are often a waste of time. Nothing useful comes out of them and people leave feeling frustrated. Unlike other, less formal conversations, meetings can create bad feeling. Participants may sense that, because the natural rules of conversation don't apply, they have licence to behave badly. Interrupting, multiple conversations, unnatural silences, aggressive argument – all now become fair play. No wonder that so many younger people, entering the business world for the first time, find meetings confrontational.

Confrontation and debate

Confrontation, indeed, becomes a common default mode when conversational rules break down. It would not be surprising, in a meeting where the natural protocols of conversation are under strain, for people to resort to aggressive or defensive behaviour.

In addition, most of us are better at advocacy than at inquiry:

we have been trained in the techniques of presenting, explaining and influencing. Our education mostly stresses the value of *arguing*: taking a position, holding it, defending it, convincing others of its worth and attacking any argument that threatens it. No wonder, then, that conversations in meetings sometimes become less a dance than a boxing match.

Four types of adversarial thinking

Edward de Bono has coined the term 'adversarial thinking' for this kind of behaviour. He suggests that it usually appears in one of four forms.

Critical thinking

For most of us, to think about something automatically means looking for something wrong with it. Take note next time you ask anybody for their response to an issue: invariably their first thoughts will be critical.

The rationale behind critical thinking is that, by looking for the weaknesses in an idea, we can strengthen it. But we rarely receive criticism in this way; instead, we try to defend our idea from the criticism, or attack the criticism itself in an effort to discredit it.

Ego thinking

In adversarial thinking, we become identified with our ideas. Criticism of an idea quickly becomes an attack on the person holding it. Debate becomes a pretext for scoring points against others. Reason gets infected with emotion.

Meetings often devote enormous amounts of energy to *preventing* emotion from overwhelming debate, but the dynamic of debate makes emotional conflict inevitable.

Rigid thinking

All thinking starts from assumptions. We can't think without first assuming something. Debate merely pits these assumptions against each other. Because they are assumed, they are rarely stated – which makes them difficult to challenge or knock down. Whoever wins the debate, the assumptions lying behind the ideas will survive – on *both* sides. As a result, our thinking becomes rigid. Any thinking that questions an assumption, or strays beyond its boundaries, can be dismissed as 'irrelevant' (or 'deviant'). Indeed, debate actually serves to *entrench* assumptions – thereby prolong the conflict.

Rigid thinking often results from:

- **conforming to authority ('if senior management see it this way, it must be right');**
- **the influence of custom ('our profession has thought like this for the past 200 years');**
- **habit ('this is the way we think around here');**
- **wilful ignorance ('thinking like this saves us the bother of dealing with inconvenient detail or finding out more').**

Political thinking

All thinking in groups tends to become political. Political thinking connects ideas to the people holding them; once an idea becomes identified with an individual, we realise that winning the debate means allying ourselves to the person as well as the idea. Simon Meijlink feels that the political climate in meetings has shifted – at least, in his own culture. 'In the Netherlands,' he says, 'I would say that meeting structures are following politics... In the last couple of decades, the "left-wing" approach of "let's discuss and get to consensus" has dramatically moved towards a more British army-style approach.'

The political style of a meeting will affect the relationships between ideas and people. To attack an idea may mean attacking its sponsor; to support it may be to create an alliance. As politics comes into play, we begin to use conversational gambits, ploys, manoeuvres and defence mechanisms, not to develop the conversation but to play politics: creating 'power bases' and undermining 'opponents', bureaucratic conniving, and behind-the-scenes manipulation.

Adversarial thinking, like other kinds of conflict, feeds on itself. Being attacked for our ideas causes pain; we respond in kind and help to prolong the conflict. We may engage in 'pre-emptive strikes', attacking before being attacked. Adversarial thinking expresses our lack of security, and the need to protect ourselves from future threats. We become locked in a 'cold war' of argument and counter-argument. Although we may recognise that our behaviour is unproductive, we feel we cannot do anything different. We do not know how to, and we may be too frightened to try.

The 'debate' myth

In an attempt to manage adversarial thinking, we have invented debate (from the Latin, 'to beat down').

Debate may be the only kind of disciplined conversation that any of us have learnt. In a debate, two ideas are set against each other. Each idea tries to discredit the other. We label the idea left standing at the end of the debate 'correct'. For debate to be effective, we must manage our ideas very strictly. Only two can be allowed at a time; the two ideas chosen must be opposed in some way.

Management gurus often make much of debate's virtues. It's said to be not merely unavoidable in business, but positively desirable. Yet debate, with its clash of divergent opinions, makes it impossible for us to consider the competing alternatives seriously. After all, *neither* idea might be correct; *both* may be partially correct. There may be lots of other ideas that might be valuable to explore. Debate cannot allow us to consider any of these possibilities. We're too busy trying to prove the opposing idea wrong to think more effectively. Often, we're too busy defending ourselves.

A debate is a conflict of rigid opinions. Opinions are ideas gone cold. They're our assumptions about what might, or should, be true, rather than what's true in specific circumstances. They may take the form of:

- **stories (about what happened, what may have happened, why it may have happened);**
- **explanations (for why something went wrong or why we failed);**
- **justifications (for taking action or not); or**
- **generalisations (to save us the trouble of thinking).**

We're so used to voicing and listening to opinions that we can easily mistake them for the truth. Whenever you hear the word 'fact' in a meeting, you can be almost certain that somebody is voicing an opinion.

The seven skills of effective conversation

How, then, can we improve the quality of the conversation in our meetings?

First: limit the number of participants. As we've seen, the normal rules of conversation will work successfully only with small groups of up to about four people. Meetings of this size are more likely to be productive because individuals have more opportunity to contribute and the group is easier to manage. In larger groups, the Chair will need to use more or less formal control techniques to help the conversation become more effective.

Here are seven more strategies for improving the conversations in meetings:

- **Improve your listening skills.**
- **Structure your thinking.**
- **Manage your time.**

- **Find common ground.**
- **Move beyond argument.**
- **Summarise often.**
- **Use visuals.**

Improve your listening skills

The quality of any conversation depends on the quality of our listening.

Listening is far more than simply not speaking. Listeners controls a speaker's behaviour by their own: by maintaining or breaking eye contact, by their body position, by nodding or shaking their head, by taking notes or doodling, and so on. Similarly, when we speak, we demonstrate the quality of our listening. If we interrupt, we demonstrate that we have stopped listening, that we are not interested in listening any longer. This, in turn, will affect the other's speaking and listening.

We all know the symptoms of poor listening. They're so familiar that we even expect them and develop tactics to cope with them: condemnation of an idea the speaker hasn't uttered, an irrelevant response, interrupting. Most of us, however, can listen effectively. We do listen well when we admire the other person or want to trip them up, when we think we might gain from what they're saying, or if we genuinely respect the speaker. And we can also listen well if we have learnt that effective listening improves group behaviour and improves a meeting's results.

The first step in improving our listening skills is to become aware of the obstacles. Some we have control over; others we may have to endure. Any conversation consists, for each participant, of two conversations: the external conversation and the internal conversation we hold inside our own heads. We must listen to both, and take note of both. As we participate in the external conversation, we may be using our internal conversation to:

- suggest answers to problems;
- develop solutions;
- rehearse our next remark; or
- judge what the speaker is saying.

At times, we should resolutely *stop* holding our inner conversation and listen – truly listen – to what the speaker is saying, to what they are not saying, and how they are saying or not saying it. At other times, we can manage the internal conversation by:

- taking notes of our thoughts so that we can put them to one side;
- making it part of the external conversation by vocalising our thoughts;
- pausing before we speak, to allow the internal conversation to happen.

Managing the inner conversation will allow us to listen more actively in the external conversation.

Structure your thinking

A group thinking together needs to know what sort of thinking it should be engaged in. Yet most of us have had little training in the skills of structured thinking. A little simple discipline can make a huge difference.

The simplest form of discipline breaks a conversation into two parts:

- *First-stage thinking* explores reality and names it. It translates what we experience into ideas.
- *Second-stage thinking* then manipulates those ideas to achieve a result. Put simply, first-stage thinking is thinking about a problem; second-stage thinking is thinking about a solution.

I sometimes think that we are obsessed with solutions. Many meetings leap to second-stage thinking without spending nearly enough time in the first stage. We look for solutions and often almost forget the problem.

Why this urge to ignore the problem? Perhaps because problems frighten us. To stay with a problem – to explore it, to try to understand it further, to confront it and live with it for a few moments – is too uncomfortable. We don't like living with an unresolved problem. Better to deal with it: sort it out, solve it.

Give the first stage – the problem stage – as much attention and time as you think appropriate. Then give it a little more. Resist the temptation to rush into second-stage thinking. And make sure that you are all in the same stage of the conversation at the same time.

Chapter 6 develops the idea of two-stage thinking further.

Manage your time

Conversations take time and time is the one entirely non-renewable resource. Manage time well, both for and in your conversations. We can manage time both *for* the conversation and *in* the conversation.

Once again, the agenda can be of great help. Allocating timings to each agenda item certainly helps us to decide how much time an issue should be allowed. Keeping to those timings also challenges us to manage the pace of the conversation.

Most conversations proceed at a varying rate. Generally, an effective conversation will probably start quite slowly and get faster as it goes on. But there are no real rules about this. You know that a conversation is going too fast when people interrupt each other a lot, when parallel conversations start, when people stop listening to each other and show signs of becoming uncomfortable. Conversely, you know that a conversation is slowing down when one person starts to dominate the conversation, when questions dry up, when people pause a lot, when the energy level in the conversation starts to drop or when people show signs of weariness.

Find common ground

Conversations are ways of finding common ground. We mostly begin conversations in our own private territory and use the conversation to find boundaries and the openings where we can cross onto the other person's ground.

We ask for, and give, permission for these moves to happen. If we are asking permission to move into new territory, we might:

- **make a remark tentatively;**
- **express ourselves with lots of hesitant padding: 'perhaps we might…', 'I suppose I think…', 'It's possible that…'; or**
- **pause before speaking.**

We shouldn't proceed until the other person has given us permission. Such permission may be explicit: 'please say what you like,' 'I would really welcome your honest opinion,' 'I don't mind you talking about that.' Other signs of permission might be in the person's body language or behaviour: nodding, smiling, leaning forward.

Conversely, refusing permission can be explicit – 'I'd rather we didn't talk about this' – or in code. The person may evade your question, wrap up an answer in clouds of mystification or reply with another question. Their non-verbal behaviour is more likely to give you a hint of their real feelings: folding their arms, sitting back in the chair, becoming restless, evading eye contact.

Move beyond argument

Breaking the cycle of conflict is a key skill in improving our conversations in meetings. The Ladder of Inference is a useful tool in helping us to develop that skill.

The model was developed initially by Chris Argyris. He pictures the way we think in conversations as a ladder. At the bottom of the ladder is observation; at the top, action:

- **From our observation, we step onto the first rung of the ladder by selecting data. (We choose what to look at.)**
- **On the second rung, we infer meaning from our experience of similar data.**
- **On the third rung, we generalise those meanings into assumptions.**
- **On the fourth rung, we construct mental models (or beliefs) out of those assumptions.**
- **We act on the basis of our mental models.**

We travel up and down this ladder whenever we hold a conversation. We are much better at climbing up than stepping down. In fact, we can leap up all the rungs in a few seconds. These 'leaps of abstraction' allow us to act more quickly but they can also limit the course of the conversation. Even more worryingly, our mental models help us to select data from future observation, further limiting the range of the conversation. Argyris calls this a 'reflexive loop'; we might call it a mindset.

The Ladder of Inference gives us more choices about where to go in a conversation. It slows down our thinking. It allows us to:

- **become more aware of our own thinking;**
- **make that thinking available to the other person;**
- **ask them about their thinking.**

Above all, it allows us to defuse an adversarial conversation by 'climbing down' from private beliefs, assumptions and opinions and then 'climbing up' to shared meanings and beliefs.

The key to using the Ladder of Inference is to ask questions. It helps us, not to score points, but to find the genuine differences in the way we think, what we have in common and how we might reach shared understanding:

- 'What's the data that underlies what you've said?'
- 'Do we agree on the data?'
- 'Do we agree on what they mean?'
- 'Can you take me through your reasoning?'
- 'When you say [what you've said], do you mean [my rewording of it]?'

For example, if one of us suggests a course of action, the other can carefully climb down the ladder by asking:

- 'Why do you think this might work?' 'What makes this a good plan?'
- 'What assumptions do you think you might be making?' 'Have you considered...?'
- 'How would this affect...?' 'Does this mean that...?'
- 'Can you give me an example?' 'What led you to look at this in particular?'

Even more powerfully, the Ladder of Inference can help us offer our own thinking for the other person to examine. If we are suggesting a plan of action, we can ask them:

- 'Can you see any flaws in my thinking?'
- 'Would you look at this stuff differently?' 'How would you put this together?'
- 'Would this look different in different circumstances?' 'Are my assumptions valid?'
- 'Have I missed anything?'

The beauty of this model is that you need no special training to use it. Neither does the other participant in the conversation. You can use it immediately, as a practical way to intervene in conversations that are descending into argument.

Summarise often

Summarising is perhaps the most important conversation skill to develop. Summaries help us to do everything else we have been discussing in this section.

Why summarise?

- **Summaries allow us to state our objective, return to it and check that we have achieved it.**
- **Summaries help us to structure our thinking, by recalling where we are in the two stages of thinking, which conversation stage we have reached and where we now need to go.**
- **Summaries help us to manage time more effectively by keeping us from digressing and moving the conversation on when necessary.**
- **Summaries help us to seek the common ground between us. By summarising what the other person is saying in our own words, we find our own way of inhabiting their territory.**
- **Summaries help us to move beyond adversarial thinking. It's simply harder to disagree with the last remark if you have to summarise it first.**

Simple summaries are useful at key turning points in a conversation. At the start, summarise your most important point or your objective. As you want to move on from one stage to the next, summarise where you think you have both got to and check that the other person agrees with you. At the end of the conversation, summarise what you have achieved and the action steps you both need to take.

Summarising isn't merely parroting what the other person has just said. To summarise means to reinterpret their ideas in your own language. It involves:

- *recognising* the specific point they've made;

- *appreciating* the position from which they say it;
- *understanding* the beliefs that inform that position.

Recognising what someone says doesn't imply that you agree with it. It does imply that you have taken the point into account. Appreciating their feelings on the matter doesn't mean you feel the same way, but it does show that you respect those feelings. And understanding the belief may not mean that you share it, but it does indicate that you consider it important. Shared problem-solving becomes much easier if those three basic summarising tactics come into play.

Of course, summaries must be genuine. They must be supported by all the non-verbal cues that demonstrate your recognition, appreciation and understanding. And those cues will look more genuine if you actually recognise, appreciate and – at least seek to – understand.

Use visuals

Apparently we remember about 20 per cent of what we hear, and over 80 per cent of what we see. Yet many of our conversations – especially in meetings – lack this crucial visual element. If communication is the process of displaying our thinking, our conversations will certainly benefit if we can somehow help each other to see our ideas.

In fact, of course, we have lots of ways of making our ideas visible in conversations. We gesture, or model with our hands in the air; we move our bodies around and express our feelings about ideas by contorting our facial muscles. There are indeed lots of other ways in which we can make our thinking visible. The obvious ways include scribbling on the nearest bit of paper or using a flip chart. Less obvious – but possibly more powerful – are word pictures: the images we can create in each other's minds with the words we use.

Metaphors are images of ideas in concrete form. The word means transferring or carrying over. A metaphor carries your meaning from one thing to another. It enables your listener to see something in a new way by picturing it as something else. Metaphor uses the imagination to support and develop your ideas.

Analogies perform much the same function as metaphors. Analogies tell us that one thing is *like* another; metaphors tell us that one thing actually is another. If I say that our competitors are forcing us to change our strategy 'like a goalie moving the goalpost', I'm using an analogy. If I say, more simply, 'our competitors are shifting the goalposts', I'm using a metaphor. Metaphor is usually a more powerful way of transforming your idea into an image than analogy.

Metaphors bring meaning alive in the listener's mind. They narrow our focus and direct our attention to what the speaker wants us to see. They stir our feelings. Metaphor can build our commitment to another person's ideas and help us to remember them.

If you want to find a metaphor to make your thinking more creative and your conversations more interesting, you might start by simply listening out for them in the conversation you are holding. We use many metaphors without even noticing them. If you are still looking, you might try asking some simple questions:

- **What's the problem like?**
- **If this were a different situation – a game of cricket, a medieval castle, a mission to Mars, a kindergarten – how would we deal with it?**
- **How would a different kind of person manage the issue: a gardener, a politician, an engineer, a hairdresser, an actor?**
- **What does this situation *feel* like?**
- **If this problem were an animal, what species of animal would it be?**
- **Describe what's going on as if it were in the human body.**

Explore your answers to these questions and develop the images that spring to mind. You need to be in a calm, receptive frame of mind to do this: the conversation needs to slow down and reflect on its own progress. Finding metaphors is very much part of first-stage thinking, because metaphors are tools to help us see reality in new ways.

You will know when you've hit on a productive metaphor. The conversation will suddenly catch fire (that's a metaphor!). You will feel a sudden injection of energy and excitement as you realise that you are thinking in a completely new way.

Along with gestures, body movement and metaphor, we have a range of technologies available to help us visualise our ideas. In my experience, conversations nearly always benefit from being recorded visually. The patterns and pictures and diagrams and doodles that we scribble on a pad help us to listen, to summarise and to keep track of what we've covered. Scale those technologies up to include flip charts and whiteboards – many of which are now interactive – and we have technologies to help larger groups focus their thinking and become more creative. Recording ideas visually also makes conversations more democratic, by making ideas the property of the group rather than any one individual. And that helps to reduce conflict and enhance innovation.

Chapter 6 contains more material on making our thinking visible.

4

Preparing for the meeting

Ninety per cent of an effective meeting happens before it takes place. Even the briefest or most informal meeting benefits from preparation, if only as a few notes scribbled on the back of an envelope. As we've seen, the potential for ineffective conversation increases with the number of people involved. Any meeting of more than five or six people will need some formal organisation.

Three key roles

Many managers claim that they have to manage too many aspects of the meeting themselves. The person who called the meeting has to cope with leading, participating in the decision-making process and trying valiantly to make notes or take minutes at the same time.

Such multitasking may be unavoidable. As organisations strive for greater efficiencies, managers are spreading their responsibilities further – and many have lost valuable secretarial support. For meetings of three or four people, the problem may not be too great. With larger groups, however, allocating responsibilities formally is probably the only way to ensure that the meeting runs efficiently *and* effectively.

We can identify three formal roles in most meetings. Although real life often forces one person to share two – or even all – of these roles, in the best meetings they are taken by different people.

Chair

The Chair has called the meeting and will lead it. Call them the meeting leader or facilitator: they take final responsibility for the meeting's success. They're often the most senior manager present, and may be the principal decision-maker.

Consequently, Chairs are often tempted to do too much: to manage the traffic of ideas while taking responsibility for the meeting's output. Vincent Nolan, a consultant with decades of experience in this area, says that combining these two functions makes the Chair into 'a sort of combined poacher and gamekeeper who cannot do both jobs well'. Some Chairs see it as their responsibility – indeed, their right – to 'steer' the meeting: to manipulate the group's thinking towards their own preferred decision. Perhaps they've learned this directorial style by observing their predecessors; they probably fail to understand how demotivating and frustrating such a style can be.

For Nolan, separating the functions of 'process management' and 'content direction' is crucial to the success of chairing. 'We do not give the job of referee to one of the players in a football match,' he says. Of course a meeting must be planned and the conversation guided towards desired outcomes. But controlling the *process* of the conversation is not the same as controlling the *task*. Process management is 'air traffic control': the complex job of listening to and guiding the conversation. Task control is like flying an aircraft to its destination: defining the task, managing information, solving problems and making decisions.

The most effective Chairs are air-traffic controllers. They set the parameters of the conversation, specify the meeting's agenda and indicate how the group should behave.

Administrator

The administrator – a term I much prefer to 'secretary' or 'minute-taker' – looks after the meeting's logistics. The administrator is principally responsible for taking an accurate record of the meeting: what happens, what is discussed, what is decided and what actions are agreed. But they often take on other responsibilities: preparation for the meeting, arrangements during the meeting and follow-up after it.

The administrator can contribute powerfully to a meeting's success. They can take over critical tasks from the Chair: summarising agenda items before discussion and summarising the discussion after each item; keeping time; even, on occasions, intervening to maintain order.

The key to developing the administrator's role is to create a close working relationship with the Chair. That may be easier said than done: some administrators work for multiple Chairs; some committee secretaries meet the Chair only in the meeting room. But delegating just a few procedural responsibilities will often show the Chair just how useful an ally the administrator can be.

Participant

Anyone at the meeting who isn't the Chair or the administrator is – or should be – a participant. They are, in Vincent Nolan's terms, 'content directors' responsible for specifying the subjects to be discussed and contributing their thinking skills to the meeting. I like the term 'task owner': each participant should have a job to do in the meeting, for which they take primary responsibility.

The best candidate for task owner is the person whose job

or work is most closely affected by the item under discussion. They're best placed to specify what to discuss, what information they need, what they expect the group to contribute and what kind of outcome they're seeking. Other participants can then act as 'thinking resources', contributing ideas and analysis as required.

Effective meetings: three key roles

Chair	*Process director*	Controls communications traffic
		Manages time
		Manages social objectives
		Oversees group development
		Specifies meeting structure
		Controls conversation
		Specifies how the group is to think
		Summarises and reflects the group's thinking
Administrator	*Recorder*	Records meeting
		Can help with time management
		Can help to maintain order in the interests of a clear record
		Can summarise at the end of agenda items and at the end of the meeting
Participant	*Task owner*	Sets objective of thinking process
		Presents relevant information
		States when task is achieved
		Measures success of outcomes
	Thinking resource	Contributes ideas or information
		Helps in thinking and solving problems
		A 'consultant' to the task owner

Preparing to chair

As Chair, then, think of yourself as an 'air-traffic controller'. As we have seen in Chapter 2, your style of control may depend on the maturity of the group you are managing: groups at the 'forming' stage may need firm direction; a high-performing group will benefit from a much lighter touch.

You may feel that the hardest task in taking on this role is to relinquish some aspects of your managerial persona. But then, chairing a meeting can be an ideal opportunity to demonstrate your managerial style. It's in meetings, more than anywhere else, that managers can show what kind of manager they are.

Clarifying your objectives

Establish the purpose of the meeting. Don't trust to imagination or memory. Write it down: this will form the basis of the meeting's title.

> I am calling this meeting to...

Your statement of purpose should revolve around a verb. What are you going to do – apart from talk? If you're going to address a number of tasks, they should be connected in some way. Are they all relevant to all the members of the group? Is the meeting necessary to carry them all out? Some tasks might be dealt with more efficiently in 'mini-meetings' before or after the main meeting, without wasting the whole group's time.

What do you want to achieve? Perhaps you will need to consider:

- **the ideal outcome;**
- **the realistic outcome;**
- **a fallback position.**

What decisions need to be taken in the meeting? Who will take them? Why must the decision be made *at the meeting*? Are resources available to carry out any actions that you anticipate emerging from the meeting? Is anybody else going to be affected? Should you perhaps consult those people – or even invite them to the meeting?

Assembling an agenda

Every meeting has an agenda. Many have more than one agenda running at the same time! The agenda may not have been written down, discussed or even thought about. But it exists, all the same. And whoever controls the agenda controls the meeting.

The most effective agendas are public and written down. If the agenda remains unclear to the whole group, the meeting may be hijacked by private agendas. Result? Confusion, frustration and failure.

The final responsibility for setting the agenda is the Chair's. After all, it's the Chair who is calling the meeting. Keep it simple. The more complicated your agenda, the more likely it will be that the meeting will flounder.

Why have an agenda?

A written agenda allows everyone to focus on what they are to do before, during and after the meeting. It acts as:

- **a plan of the meeting to aid preparation;**
- **an objective control of the meeting's progress;**
- **a measure of the meeting's success.**

The word 'agenda' is Latin for 'things to be done'. An agenda should not be a list of subject headings. Each agenda item should be an instruction. It should tell the participants:

- **what the task is;**
- **how it will be tackled;**
- **what the group will do at the end of the item.**

Every item on the agenda should contain at least one verb, indicating what the group will do.

> 'Item 7: New IT network'

says very little that will help participants to prepare. Verbs can clearly indicate what kind of thinking you're expecting at that point in the meeting.

> 'Item 3: New IT network. Clive to present quotations and essential specifications of systems under consideration. Team to agree system to be recommended for purchase.'

This much fuller entry indicates what the group is to do, who has a key responsibility in carrying out the task, and how we will know whether we have achieved our objective.

Contents of an agenda: checklist

The most formal agendas will include (in this order):

- title of meeting;
- date, time, venue;
- apologies for absence;
- minutes of previous meeting;
- matters arising from the previous meeting;
- other items to be discussed and decided;
- motions relating to the above;
- reports from sub-committees;
- contributions from guest speakers;
- any other business;
- date, time and venue of next meeting

Your agenda may not need to be so comprehensive. Consider the advantages of including timings for each item and 'owners' for each item.

Constructing the agenda

As you gather items for the agenda, look for:

- **a logical order;**
- **a common thread (keep linked items together);**
- **routine items (place near the beginning);**
- **special factors (for example, people who are only involved in a part of the meeting);**
- **difficult or contentious items.**

The agenda should follow a natural shape. The most 'difficult' items – those needing the most discussion and thinking work – can be best placed in the middle third of the meeting, when the group's physical and mental alertness are at their peak. Routine items, information items or urgent matters that can be dealt with quickly, can be put first; and the 'easiest' items – those of greatest interest, or presentations by guest speakers – towards the end.

The agenda should also reflect the thinking process that you wish to follow. We'll investigate how groups can think more effectively together in Chapter 6.

Assembling the agenda items

- **Remove any unnecessary items.**
- **Give detailed titles to each item.**
- **Every title should contain at least one verb: what the group will *do*.**
- **Give timings to each item.**
- **Indicate any specific speakers to an item.**
- **Note any attached papers – in case of loss.**
- **Consider putting motions on a separate sheet, for ease of reference.**

Beware of 'Any other business'! If something is worth discussing, it should be itemised on the agenda. All too often, people use 'AOB' to pursue private or hidden agendas, to settle old scores, reawaken old grudges or make lengthy and irrelevant complaints. If you can, remove this item from the agenda. Your meeting should end on a positive note, with a summary of what you have achieved and the suggested next steps.

How to avoid 'any other business'

- Distribute a draft agenda, with invitations for contributions.
- Invite participants to submit any late business at the start of the meeting.
- Decide whether to include extra items on the basis of their urgency, not their importance. Make it clear that any late inclusions are at the Chair's discretion.
- Amend the agenda. Consider placing the new items at the beginning of the meeting, rather than at the end.
- Allocate time to the new items and revise the timings for the rest of the agenda. Keep to the original overall timing of the meeting; simply extending it is counterproductive.

Watching the clock

Timing the length of agenda items may depend on when you schedule it. Tackling a problem too soon may lead to much unnecessary discussion (delay the conversation and the problem may just solve itself). Think also about the time of day when you will be meeting. Research suggests that the best time for thinking is late morning: a finding confirmed by the international air company that made it policy a few years ago for all meetings to be held in one of two slots: 9–11 am and 11 am–1 pm. Consider, also, other ways to save time. It may be possible, for example, to arrange the meeting in conjunction with others.

Are your meetings too long? It's a recurrent complaint. Some Chairs seem to make it a point of honour to have meetings that last for hours. But longer doesn't mean better. A successful meeting depends on how much – and how well – everybody participates, not on how long it is.

Here's the golden rule:

No meeting, or part of a meeting, should last longer than 90 minutes.

If you *must* go on longer – because you are gathering a group from far and wide, for example – include time for breaks, refreshments and mental recuperation.

Incredibly, many meetings still begin without any agreed finishing time. 'We just go on until we've finished,' sighs the beleaguered Chair. Nothing does more harm to concentration and discipline than an open-ended meeting. The agenda should announce a finishing time – and the Chair should keep to it.

Even the most effective Chairs can sometimes be agreeably surprised at how efficient meetings can be. Professor David Baulcombe, Regius Professor of Botany at Cambridge University, prides himself on keeping administrative meetings as short as possible. 'However,' he wrote recently, 'I hear that, in my absence, a recent departmental meeting was over in 50 minutes – 10 minutes less than normal.' Professor Baulcombe is encouraged by the news. 'I am sure I can cut this down even more and plan to take the chairs out of our meeting room so that, like the Privy Council, we stand for the meeting.'

Less is more. *Fit the items on the agenda to the available time* – and not the other way around. A group can perform well only for so long: the more you try to pack on to your agenda, the less you will achieve. Timings for individual items are useful here: if you find you can allocate only a few minutes to an important item, you are overfilling the agenda. Always be on the lookout, too, for unnecessary items that can be dealt with outside the meeting.

When you have finalised the timings of the agenda items, try something radical. *Cut all the timings by 50 per cent.* You might be surprised at how pressure of time concentrates minds and energises your meeting.

And if your meetings are *still* lasting too long, work out the cost. Download a Meeting Cost Clock and calculate the money your organisation is spending on each meeting!

Making your meeting shorter

- Announce a finishing time. It's discourteous not to.
- Limit the number of items on the agenda to the time allowed.
- Allocate a task owner to each item, who will take responsibility for any decision.
- Impose a time limit on each agenda item.
- Allow time for breaks.
- Prepare procedures for unresolved business.
- Make it your goal to end on time.

Who is attending?

Well: you are, for a start! But is there a good reason for you to chair? Or is it merely force of habit that puts you in this position? In regular meetings, you could rotate the role – either from meeting to meeting, or even at different stages of the same meeting – so that everybody in the team has the opportunity to experience that tricky responsibility. At the very least, people may become less willing to 'misbehave' when they know that it's their turn to keep order next time!

Who are the participants in your meeting? How can you see them as 'task owners'? What's their relevance to the meeting's purpose? Are there any particular kinds of contribution you want them to make, or that they intend to make? Perhaps they are key decision-makers or experts. They may be 'thought leaders' or senior managers. They should certainly have a good reason for being there – a reason reflected somewhere on the agenda.

Are they able to attend? The more valuable they are to the meeting, the less likely they are to be available! Will a deputy or last-minute substitute be acceptable? What do they need to prepare for the meeting? Should you brief them or send them papers: the minutes of the previous meeting, reports, the latest figures?

Look over your agenda and allocate names to items. Who is the 'task owner' for each agenda item? Who will need to take the critical decision? Who will carry it through? You could ask the task owner to lead the conversation for that item, allowing you to sit back and manage the 'air space'.

Do the participants form a natural group? How well do they know each other? What are their interests, aims, ambitions and assumptions about each other? Do you envisage conflicts between any of these interests and ambitions? Where is the common ground between them?

The administrator's role

The main complaints voiced by meeting administrators are that they:

- **have been brought in at a moment's notice;**
- **are unclear what their responsibilities are;**
- **do not understand what people are talking about.**

The Chair may have to help the administrator overcome some of these problems, but the administrators themselves bear some responsibility for doing their job well.

Working with the Chair

The Chair can forestall many of these common problems at a 'pre-meeting meeting'. At this meeting, Chair and administrator can agree:

- **the purpose of the meeting;**
- **who is attending;**
- **what will go on the agenda;**
- **background information to help in taking the minutes.**

How will you record the meeting's progress? Do not be hidebound by tradition: consider how to improve the style of the minutes. Administrators will be able to take the minutes more effectively if they have the authority to:

- **intervene to clarify points that are unclear;**
- **summarise at the end of each item with details of decisions and actions agreed.**

Talk together about these matters *before the meeting*. The administrator can be invaluable in helping the Chair during the meeting to keep time, to keep to the agenda and to keep order. Taking on these responsibilities will make administering the meeting itself more satisfying.

Anticipating success: the six 'W's

Kipling's famous 'honest serving men' – the six 'W' questions – are as good a tool as any to cover most, if not all, the issues you will need to consider when preparing for a meeting.

'Why?': clarifying the purpose of the meeting with the Chair
Knowing the meeting's purpose will help the administrator

take minutes more effectively. If you have some idea what people are talking about – and, more importantly, *why* they are discussing it – you will be able to follow the conversation more fully. By understanding the goal of the conversation, you can also judge whether the conversation has arrived at a decision that meets the goal. Even if you, as administrator, are not responsible for the output of the meeting, you can help the Chair to guide the group to more specific decisions if you know what kind of decision is required.

Understanding more about the meeting's objectives will also help to make the meeting more enjoyable – or, at least, less boring – for the minute-taker.

'Who?': liaising with participants

The administrator may well need to manage arrangements with the participants in the meeting. It's probably you who will be distributing the agenda (perhaps in draft form, inviting contributions) or the minutes of the last meeting. You will also probably need to manage travel arrangements or prepare papers and presentations.

Making these connections will help you put names to faces when you are in the meeting room. Helping others will almost certainly help you.

'When': times and timings

Work with the Chair to organise both when the meeting is happening and how long it will last. Check all the item timings; do they add up to the total amount of time allocated for the meeting? Encourage the Chair to reduce the amounts of time allocated. Remind them of the cost of lengthy conversations!

'Where?': the meeting's venue

The venue can be as critical to a meeting's success as the time of day it's held. Is the venue conveniently located? Is it accessible for people with disabilities, for example, or women travelling alone at night? Are you meeting on 'home ground'? Will everybody feel at ease when they are in the room? I remember one meeting where most of us felt distinctly intimidated by the trophies of a dominant senior manager, hung around the walls. If the meeting is in a hotel or conference venue, you will need to liaise with hotel staff to establish timings, numbers, catering and needs for equipment.

Is the room the right size and shape? Is it suitable for your purpose? The Chair may wish to place allies (or potential troublemakers!) in 'control positions'. The administrator should be able to communicate easily with everybody – and especially the Chair – while taking the minutes. Everybody should be able to see a screen or flip chart with a minimum of disruption.

Effective participation depends on easy eye contact. Participants should be about one arm's length from each other. Closer, and they will invade each other's space; further apart, they will feel isolated and the group dynamics will suffer.

'How?': setting the procedure

Your procedural style will determine how the meeting – well, proceeds. What type of meeting is it? Do you have to abide by regulations or legal requirements in the way you run the meeting? How do you expect participants to contribute? How will you help the Chair control the conversation? Will everybody address their remarks, formally, through the Chair? Or perhaps you will opt for a policy of minimal control: doing no more than announcing each item, summarising discussion, calling for a formal decision – and, crucially, keeping to time.

'What?': preparing materials

The administrator has a key role in preparing the materials that will support the meeting's thinking. You may need to print and distribute papers, prepare presentations or set up equipment.

This kind of work is taking up more and more time and effort as technology races ahead. Val Tyler has noticed some of the consequences: 'minute-takers and secretaries', she says, 'are now having to manage presentations and documentation as e-mail attachments, or handed over on memory sticks – often during the meeting itself.'

Get to know how things work. Be ready to save the day when a beamer fails or if a laptop fails to connect.

Preparing to participate

Much attention is focused on the Chair's need to prepare well for a meeting. But participants too often arrive at a meeting having given little thought to how they can contribute to its success.

It's not always the fault of the participants themselves, as Val Tyler notes: 'Changes to the agenda can be notified at the last minute, leaving participants ill-prepared or lacking important information.'

The key point is to know *why* you are attending. What are you expected to contribute?

What is your role?

We have already seen (in Chapter 2) that the roles people adopt in meetings contribute to the way a group structures itself and behaves. A role is a set of behaviours by which we can help the meeting achieve its objectives.

Most of us tend to contribute to groups in consistent ways. We can broadly categorise these types as:

- **ideas people;**
- **action people;**
- **administrators;**
- **carers.**

Ideally, the group should contain a balance of all four. To adjust the balance in the group, you may need to play a certain role more strongly than normal.

Many meetings fail because the group is dominated by one or two roles. This situation often arises in teams made up of professional or technical specialists promoted to managerial positions. A group of ideas people may be enormously creative but may never get anything done. A group of action people may spend all their time arguing about what to do, pitching one solution against another without investigating causes or different perspectives on the problem. A group of administrators may pay great attention to 'the dots and commas' but fail to come up with new solutions. A group of carers may look after each other but fail to address difficult or contentious issues.

Creating a briefing paper

Briefing papers often form the basis for conversations in meetings. These may outline the issue to be discussed in some detail, give background information and indicate the preferred direction the 'task owner' would like the meeting to take. They may also form the basis of a formal presentation at the meeting.

The main risk, of course, is that the papers may not be read. The more papers the participants have, the less likely they are to read all of them. If you are writing a briefing for a meeting, you must make your paper as readable as possible and put points over as explicitly as you can.

Knowing what points to make can itself be difficult. You may not be clear what is expected of you, or what you can suggest without overstepping your authority. As a result, many briefing papers are indigestible. Using the traditional report structure – introduction, findings, conclusion, recommendations – may not help. In fact, it often results in one of two kinds of briefing paper. Avoid them at all costs!

- *The storyline*. **This is the paper that begins at the very beginning and labours heavily towards its conclusion. Writers usually justify writing storylines by asserting that the meeting 'must know all the background in** order to understand the conclusion'. In fact, readers are unlikely to bother with a narrative when they cannot see its relevance.

- *The stream of consciousness*. Here, the writer puts down thoughts in exactly the order in which they occurred. Writers will justify the stream of consciousness by saying: 'I want the reader to follow the course of my thinking.' Unfortunately, if the readers can see no *reason* to follow your reasoning, they probably will not bother to do so.

The critical point is that your paper must contain only the information necessary to support your ideas – not everything you know about the topic. An effective briefing paper is well planned. Planning the paper, like planning anything else, is a *design* process. And the design that delivers information most clearly to most readers is a pyramid.

A pyramid structure organises your ideas into a hierarchy. At the top of the pyramid is a message. This is your governing idea: the thought that you want the reader to grasp, even if they fail to read another word. The message is then supported by a small number of key points – also ideas – that explain or fill out the message in more detail. These points are then in turn supported by information that fills out your ideas still further.

Here's how to build your pyramid structure:

- *Establish the purpose of the paper*. What are you trying to achieve in this paper? Most business documents seek either to persuade or to explain. Briefing papers are no different. In particular, are you making recommendations or offering options (two of the most common purposes of such papers)?
- *Think about your audience*. How will the committee, board or meeting act in response to your paper? What information do they need? What do they already know? What more do they need to know? What do they value or find important? What will convince them?

- *Work out your key message.* You should be able to express your governing idea in a simple sentence of no more than about 15 words. Place it, prominently, at the beginning of the paper, as the summary. Make sure that your message clearly expresses your purpose.
- *Work out the key points you need to make to support the message.* Each key point can form the core of a section of the paper, if necessary. Keep the number of key points small in number: no more than six, no matter how big or complicated the subject may be.
- *Throughout the paper, remember to make points and support them.* Do not give more information than is necessary to support your points; resist going into detail as much as you can. Make your style assertive and proactive.

5

Chairing the meeting

Chairing a meeting is essentially a leadership task. The Chair's job is to release the talents of the group. You should provide vision, direction and security. How you do so will depend very much on your preferred style of chairing. The best Chairs, like the best leaders, wear their authority lightly. Lao-tsu, the writer of the *Tao Te Ching*, recognised this over 2,000 years ago:

> The best soldier is not soldierly.
> The best fighter is not ferocious.
> The best conqueror does not take part in the war.
> The best employer of men keeps himself below them.
> This is called the virtue of not contending.
> This is called the ability of using people.

In other words: direct the process of the meeting; delegate task leadership to participants. Lead the operation, but don't take part.

'Air traffic control': the Chair as leader

Think of chairing, as we've said, as being akin to air traffic control. Your task is to manage the air space: to make it easier for the group to think together. Groups work best when they feel ownership of tasks, and that they are empowered to act. They will also work more efficiently if they feel secure: that somebody is in overall control.

Groups, then, have task and social objectives. You will lead, accordingly, in two dimensions: task leadership and social leadership. Task leadership is more or less directive; social leadership is more or less supportive. Tuckman's model (in Chapter 2) suggests that, as groups develop, the balance between these two kinds of leadership will tend to shift:

- *Task leadership* – **clarifying objectives, setting parameters, guiding the group in its thinking – will tend to dominate the first two stages of group development, as the group is forming and as diverse views emerge at the storming stage.**
- *Social leadership* – **helping the group to negotiate conflict and maintain coherence, establishing norms of behaviour – will tend to dominate the central stages of development, as conflicts threaten group cohesion and as the group seeks the values by which it will operate.**

Group development stage	Task direction	Group support
Forming	High	Low
Storming	High	High
Norming	Low	High
Performing	Low	Low

A group might go through all four of these stages in a single meeting. You may need to give a high level of direction at the start of the meeting, when a group is newly formed, or when the meeting is large and a high degree of procedural discipline must be invoked. You may need to explicitly support the group – praising, encouraging, thanking – in the central part of the meeting, taking more of a back seat as it moves towards its conclusion.

Opening the meeting

A meeting that starts badly will take time to recover. It's a good idea to work out an opening procedure in some detail: it will steady the nerves and put everybody at ease. Remember: high direction, low support.

- *Start on time.* **If you don't, you'll have late arrivals for the next meeting. Lateness can become a chronic problem if not dealt with immediately. Anybody who arrives late at a meeting that started promptly should soon get the message.**
- *State the purpose or objective of the meeting.* **Refer to the agenda, and indicate the common ground that exists within the group to reach this goal.**
- *Make all suitable introductions.* **Check that everybody knows each other. Attend in particular to new members.**
- *Announce procedures and the timetable of the meeting.* **Tell people how long the meeting will last, and times of breaks. Indicate how you expect them to contribute and how you intend to control the discussion.**
- *If you are chairing a new group:*
  - **Identify and agree the group's purpose.**
  - **Give information on everybody attending: their expertise and relevance to the task.**
  - **Invite everybody to introduce themselves.**

- *If the group is well established:*
  - Identify the purpose of this meeting.
  - Note any changes in circumstances since the last meeting.
  - Remind the group of its identity.
  - Introduce new members or guests.
  - Praise achievements of the group or individuals since the last meeting.
  - Acknowledge new difficulties.
  - Reaffirm the determination of the meeting to meet the challenge.

Managing agenda items

Lead by example. Keep the group focused on your vision of the meeting: not only what we want to achieve, but how we want to behave. Manage the conversation by asking questions, listening, energising, praising, accepting and, occasionally, disciplining. Check that each task leader is satisfied with the outcome: that decisions and actions, and the responsibilities and deadlines associated with them, are clear.

Take each item separately and in order. Clarify which item the meeting is addressing, and redirect participants when they stray into other items.

- Refer to the agenda.
- Do not start an item before concluding the previous one.
- Clarify the purpose of the item.
- Start the discussion positively.
- Remind the group how much time is allocated.

Ensure that the meeting doesn't waste time. Be ready to check whether the discussion is useful, or even necessary, to the task leader. Challenge gossip, in particular. Remind participants of their responsibilities to use time well. You might even record the time taken for each item against the task leader's name: this can work wonders for group discipline!

Encouraging contributions

Most of us sometimes need to be encouraged to speak out. An important idea may never emerge because somebody is too reticent or overawed to volunteer it. Meetings can easily become 'tennis matches' dominated by a few strong personalities while everybody else looks on helplessly. The Chair can encourage democracy in two ways:

- *Task behaviour*. **Initiating discussion, building on it, making suggestions.**
- *Process behaviour*. **Gate-keeping to allow everyone to contribute, time-keeping to concentrate people's minds, and summarising the group's feelings.**

Everybody should feel relaxed about contributing, and that their contribution is valued. Distinguish contributions from the people making them. Praise useful ideas and remarks rather than according the speaker gushing adoration; be critical, if you must, of a comment without condemning the speaker. Be open, honest and *specific*.

Using questions and statements

At the next meeting you attend, count the number of questions. Compare it to the number of assertions made. What conclusions can you draw?

Managers are often dismayed at the lack of questions in meetings they chair. Perhaps they have forgotten how politically charged questions can be. In many organisations, to question is simply 'not done'. 'Questioning', wrote Samuel Johnson with typically heavy irony, 'is not the mode of conversation among gentlemen.' As a result, many managers become much more skilled in advocating their own ideas than in enquiring into those of others – or into their own.

We ask questions to find out, to check our understanding and – if we are good questioners – to help others improve their understanding. But we also question for many other reasons: to ridicule someone, to criticise or to make ourselves look clever. We need to make sure that we're asking questions for the right reasons.

Become aware of the repertoire of questions available to you. Use them to help you pilot the conversation: to open it, keep it alive, take it in new directions, steer it away from dangerous waters or shallows where it might get stuck, and bring it to a close.

Ask genuine questions, truly seeking information, encouraging people to speak from their experience and expertise, rather than 'putting answers into their mouths'.

Types of question

Closed (can only be answered 'yes' or 'no')	*'Can you...?', Will you...?', 'Is it...?', 'Do you...?*	Gets a 'yes' or 'no'. Establishes matters of fact. Focuses the discussion. Stops rambling. Checks understanding.
Open (cannot be answered 'yes' or 'no')	*'Why/what/who/ where/when/how?'*	Avoids 'yes' or 'no'. Opens up discussion. Encourages a contribution. Gains information in a non-directive way. Gets ideas.

Specific	*'At what point...?', Where exactly...?'*	Directs the discussion. Prevents rambling. Engages expertise. Brings people into the conversation. Speeds up and focuses attention.
Overhead	*'What do we all think?'*	Addresses the group. Helps to avoid embarrassment. Stimulates answers from newcomers. Can help to make a point without sacrificing impartiality.
Relay	*'Thanks Nadeem. Tony, what do you think?'*	Switches from one speaker to another. Allows group to compare ideas. Keeps the conversation moving.
Reverse	*'Well: what do **you** think?'*	Reflects a question back to questioner. Encourages a speaker to expand or qualify.

Statements are useful at the beginning of a meeting, to define the purpose, objectives and scope of the conversation. Make your opening statements positive. You can use statements during agenda items to:

- *Introduce it.* **'We're all aware of the problems in this area. They include...'**

- *Give information.* 'This is a new venture for the company. Briefly it works like this...'
- *Temper conflict or confusion with fact.* 'Perhaps I can make a few points clear at this stage...'
- *Gauge the mood of the group.* 'I can see that there's a good deal of frustration about this...', 'I think we're all satisfied about that decision...', 'It seems to me that we're getting confused...'
- *Provoke, to energise or stimulate discussion.* 'Our jobs all depend on this!'

Summarising

All meetings go through periods of relative calm, between or within items. The group is uncertain of the next move; the conversation dries up, begins to go in circles or degenerates into chat. At times like this, the Chair should intervene with a summary.

Good timing is essential. Don't try to summarise when the discussion is in full swing: take notes to prepare yourself for the moment when the group stops generating ideas. There are three main points in any meeting when summarising becomes a useful tool to guide the conversation:

- *Summarising within items.* **Control contributions by summarising them when people ramble, repeat themselves or become anecdotal. Mark the end of one phase of the conversation with a summary before inviting further comments. Summarise to bring together the strands of a discussion, or when it goes slack. Sometimes a summary can be used to check how much agreement you have achieved and to reopen the discussion.**
- *Summarising at the end of items.* **This will seal an agreement or clarify exactly what has been agreed. This is a task that can usefully be given to the administrator, to help clarify what to put in the minutes.**

- *Summarising at the end of the meeting.* **A brief summary will remind the group of its achievement and point the way forward to the actions that will be taken.**

Problem people

Every meeting has them. Group members can cause problems if their individual interests come into conflict with those of the group. A basic rule is to treat problem people as members of the group, and not as troublesome individuals. But this may be easier said than done!

Problem people and how to deal with them

The bulldog	Aggressive, inflexible. Looking for a fight. Out to score points. Liable to attack without warning.	Give them a bone to chew. Separate their words from their manner. Keep cool.
The horse	Keen but boring. Goes by the book. Intelligent but could plod on forever.	Lead them to water: give them a job to do. Harness their remarks by summarising and restating.
The fox	Crafty. Undermines the meeting. Conspirational, whispers a lot. A potential hijacker.	Force them to make their views public. Look for the hidden agenda. Set the bulldog on them.
The monkey	Know-it-all. Point-of-order expert. Chatters incessantly. Swings from 'tree to tree'. Volunteers a lot.	Keep control of procedure. Ask closed questions. Give them something to. do.

The hedgehog	Prickly. Whines and whinges. Despises everybody else: may have been squashed once or twice. Sceptical, unhelpful, defensive (curls into a ball).	Tickle their belly. Respect their expertise. Ask them to help. Give them status (and a bowl of warm milk).
The gazelle	Timid and retiring. May be young. Liable to run away. A silent worrier. Unwiling to stand their ground.	Ask direct questions. Encourage. Praise. Seduce into the conversation. Protect from bulldogs.
The frog	Blabbermouth. Leaps in unthinkingly. 'Read it, read it'. Ill-informed. Puts his/her foot in it: potential victim of the fox.	Keep to the point. Appeal to the clock. Ignore their gaffes. Ask them to do the minutes.
The hippo	Wallows. Half asleep. Likes mud, and not much else. Will agree to anything. Likely to say: 'Why me?'	Try to heave them out of the mud. Pick on them suddenly. Challenge them.
The giraffe	Easily distracted. Dreams in the treetops. Rather sensitive. Will do anything not to fall over. A silent worrier.	Bring them down to earth.

Difficult situations

The meeting that goes exactly according to plan probably doesn't exist. If the Chair and participants are behaving professionally, few situations should cause major disruption. The following are perhaps the most serious.

Conflict

Conflict is undoubtedly one of the most common sources of anxiety in meetings. We saw in Chapter 3 how meetings can collapse into argument, hostility and ritual recrimination almost as a matter of course. Don't regard conflict as inevitable or desirable. You are not powerless in the face of emotional hostility; but, in order to handle it well, you need to distance yourself from it.

Begin by trying to locate the source of the problem. Sometimes this is obvious: insecurity at a time of great change, stress, a new set of working relationships or pressure from public exposure. Or it may seem to bubble up from nowhere, starting with something small and escalating quickly as it takes hold of the group. Conflict thrives on confusion and doubt. Some group members may seek to manipulate it for their own ends, or use it to justify their cynicism about all matters managerial. As conflict grows through a group, it becomes more emotional, generalised and unfocused. Looking for a target, it can find the Chair, turning the meeting into an all-purpose 'grouse session'.

Hostility often results from a sense of powerlessness. What disables us is the feeling of being at the mercy of forces outside our control. Anger often centres on what has happened in the past, and in particular on what 'they' have done: senior management, other teams, department heads, rogue operators who have bucked the system, engineers or sales staff who are never in the office, customers, suppliers, competitors...

Be prepared. If you're facing conflict or group resistance, give yourself a single overriding objective: to empower the group to do something practical. Only by focusing their thoughts on the future, and on what they can do, will you transform people's energy from conflict into purposeful activity.

- *Make the objective of the meeting clear at the outset.* Write it up on a flip chart and be ready to refer back to it frequently. Challenge people to explain the relevance of their remarks to the meeting's objectives.
- *Remember that your task is to control the conversation.* Resist being drawn into the emotional maelstrom, however hard that may be:
  - *Slow the conversation down.* Do not mirror the tone, pitch or speed of others' speech.
  - *Do not interrupt* – or cut people off in mid-sentence.
  - *Listen and record the points people make.* A flip chart or whiteboard can focus the conversation on one area and can defuse conflict effectively.
  - *Don't join in.* Do not be tempted to argue, or to contradict opinions or generalisations: about what 'they' do, or what 'always' happens. A good response to such remarks would be: 'In what circumstances does this happen?'
  - *Turn complaints into objectives.* Ask people to restate them as 'how to' statements. Write these up on the flip chart and display them.
  - *Stop people from talking about others who are not at the meeting.* Insist that 'they' are not here and we are, and that only we can address our objectives.
  - *Focus on solutions, not problems.* Think forwards, not back – and encourage the group to do the same.
  - *Be a broken record!* Repeat your questions to the group, over and over – 'What are we trying to do? What can we do about it? How does this relate to our objectives?'
  - *Be specific.* People should know what contribution they are being asked to make, and how their contribution will contribute to wider objectives. Being explicit about goals and targets is the only way

to achieve this. If you genuinely consult – asking for suggestions, inviting people to participate in finding solutions – a great deal of resistance will melt away.

- *Focus on action.* Draw the group's attention away from what others have done or are doing, towards *what we will do in the future.* You'll have to be sensitive about this. Demonstrating that you understand people's grievances can be useful in winning them over to your own ideas, and in rooting out areas for improvement. However, there will come a point in a 'grouse session' when you should start asking, insistently but quietly: 'So what are we going to do?' In this way, you'll divert attention from damaging 'storytelling' and complaint towards commitment and agreement. By showing that something can be done, you can show people that they have power to change things.

Hidden agendas

We all go to meetings with our own private agendas. They may emerge or remain hidden. They're only harmful when they come into conflict with the meeting's public agenda.

Private agendas can be productive or destructive. Good private agendas might include seeing the meeting as a career investment or encouraging participation in others. Bad private agendas include empire-building and deliberately fomenting conflict. Evidence for harmful hidden agendas might include:

- stonewalling ('I've no choice', delay, promises unfulfilled, outright refusal to act);
- attack (on every idea and everybody: insults, bullying, lots of bluster);
- trickery (denying having said something, twisting an argument, double meanings).

The most dangerous thing about a hidden agenda is that it's hidden. If you can locate the fear that causes it, you may be able to remove the agenda by removing the fear. If you can't trace suspicious tactics to their source, you may be able at least to show that you recognise the tactic. This may stop the behaviour recurring, though it may not root out the hidden agenda itself.

Don't let your suspicions become paranoia. In turning the search for hidden agendas into a witch hunt, you'll start to create your own hidden agenda.

Power games and politics

Politics are an inevitable part of our lives as members of groups. All meetings will therefore involve politics of some kind. Getting things done means wielding power. Wielding power alone, of course, does not ensure that anything useful is achieved! In some cases, calling a meeting is a sign merely that somebody has acquired enough power to call a meeting. Power games and politics express tensions and shifting relationships within the group. If you chair meetings, you'll find yourself involved in political behaviour.

You must decide how you propose to deal with it. How do you seek to influence others? What kinds of power do you have and which would you like to cultivate? How do those around you use power? How can you influence those with influence so as to align them with your objectives?

Hijacking

Hijacking is a severe loss of direction that occurs when a private agenda attempts to take over. It may even involve a conspiracy.

The Chair and other participants have a duty to rescue the meeting from hijacking. Alliances may need to be made and appeals made to the agenda. A hijack by definition is by one person or by a minority. Appeals to group solidarity should be sufficient to solve the problem, at least temporarily. An attempted hijack usually means that a major issue needs to be addressed: a period of storming may ensue.

Senior management are liable to hijack meetings chaired by

subordinates. The Chair must exercise proper authority. If the meeting is conducted properly and fairly, they will have nothing to fear from a responsible senior manager – who may after all be assessing their leadership potential.

Groupthink

In the 1960s, Irving Janis studied a number of disastrous American foreign policy decisions, including the Bay of Pigs. He attributed these poor decisions to 'groupthink'. (The term had been coined a decade earlier, but Janis made it famous.) Janis defined groupthink as 'the psychological drive for consensus at any cost that suppresses dissent and appraisal of alternatives in cohesive decision-making groups'.

Groupthink results from a group's pursuit of social cohesion. It's often a strong indication that the group has reached the norming stage of development. At this point, group members self-censor contributions that the group might interpret as 'deviant' from its norms. As a result, the meeting's thinking becomes dangerously limited to what the group allows.

Symptoms of groupthink include the illusion of invulnerability and an unthinking sense of unanimity. The consequences can be a severe limitation of thinking in the meeting, a misjudgement of risk and wilfully ignoring alternative points of view.

To counteract groupthink:

- **Challenge the need for collective decision-making and appoint 'decision owners'; encourage diverse opinions systematically.**
- **Appoint one person in the group as 'devil's advocate', to evaluate all contributions critically.**
- **Pursue disagreements in an orderly way.**
- **Invite outsiders or new group members to 'kick-start' change.**
- **Ensure that task leaders or process directors are willing to have their own judgements examined critically.**

- Examine the procedures of the group: how often you meet, how long since you changed personnel, whether you act democratically.

Closing the meeting

Closing the meeting well is as important as opening it well. The group is about to disperse. We should show everyone what they have achieved, acknowledge their success and thank them for their efforts. And we must also make sure that people commit to taking action.

Chapter 6 contains more details about gaining commitment to actions at the end of a meeting. It's important to delegate as many actions as possible (or, ideally, all of them). This will relieve you of some of the burden, give participants ownership of the actions agreed and demonstrate trust.

All agreed actions should have specific, named 'actioners', who should feel that they 'own' the action. They should understand why they are doing it and have the authority and resources to carry it through. Make sure that nobody takes on an unrealistic amount of work. Schedule actions to happen as soon as possible. Participants are more likely to take prompt action if they are still fired with enthusiasm by the meeting they have just left.

Back up all decisions and actions in writing. A summary action sheet distributed with (or before) the full minutes can be useful. Others affected by the action may need to be contacted by memo or e-mail.

- **Summarise what has been decided and point the way ahead.**
- **Briefly announce what actions are to occur: by whom and when.**
- **Test for commitment.**

- **Check that the administrator is happy with the record of the meeting.**
- **Set the time and date of the next meeting if possible.**
- **End positively. Emphasise the achievements of the meeting.**
- **Thank everybody for their attendance and their contributions.**

You may think that the meeting is over as soon as it finishes. But there will be usually be more to do. The minutes, for one thing, will need to be produced. Do you have an efficient process for issuing them? And most actions will need to be followed up at the appropriate time. If 'actioners' have not done what they committed to by the agreed deadline, you may need to do more than complain. Ask why things have not been done. Maybe the 'actioner' was over-enthusiastic and took on too much; maybe the action itself was unrealistic.

Meetings are rarely single events. Often, they are part of a cycle of activity: a meeting leads to action, which provokes change, which itself must be evaluated or responded to – usually by calling another meeting! As the Chair, your responsibility for holding successful meetings is almost certainly closely connected to your wider responsibilities as a manager and leader. It's in meetings that you have the opportunity to exercise those responsibilities publicly.

6

Improving the group's thinking

We're paid to think. Our success depends on our results; we think when we want results that are better than they would be without thinking. Yet most of us aren't trained to think. Thinking isn't yet regarded as a key managerial skill: it's rarely listed, for example, as a core competence.

Because we rarely think about thinking as a skill, we've developed a number of damaging misconceptions about it that we should dispel.

- *Thinking is not an alternative to doing.* **We can use thinking as an excuse not to act; and we can act without thinking. The reason we do both so much is that we regard thinking and action as opposed. They are not. Effective thinking improves the effectiveness of our actions; and our actions are a rich source of good ideas.**
- *Thinking is not intelligence.* **Thinking unintelligently may still achieve something. Intelligence without thinking is useless.**

- *Thinking is not a function of education.* Highly educated people are not necessarily good thinkers, and many people with little education can think extremely effectively.
- *Thinking is not being clever.* Increasing our knowledge isn't thinking: it's simply hoarding. Too much information can seriously hamper our ability to think.
- *Thinking is not only the operation of logic.* It involves looking, exploring, choosing, designing, evaluating and having hunches. It includes considering priorities, objectives, alternatives, consequences and other people's opinions.

There's a Japanese proverb: 'None of us is as smart as all of us.' Yet most groups of people think far less well than any one of them individually. Why should this be?

- *We confuse conversation about the task with conversation about process.* We identify thoughts with people. We talk in code. We use conversation to express loyalties or alliances, to bid for power, to protect our position or sense of self-worth. We persist in old conventions or habits of conversation to feel more comfortable.
- *We fail to manage the structure of the conversation.* A well-managed conversation will begin with clear objectives and end with clear actions. Many conversations have unclear agendas (or hidden agendas); others are combinations of several conversations at once. We allow our conversations to ramble, to get stuck, to be hijacked or stifled. Because the behavioural or 'political' aspects of conversation are so powerful, we find it difficult to influence the course of conversations productively – particularly in a meeting, when a group of people are involved.

We need to tackle these two failings if we want to help ourselves think better in meetings.

First-stage thinking and second-stage thinking

We can imagine thinking as a process in two stages. First-stage thinking is perception; second-stage thinking is judgement. We do first-stage thinking when we're working out what we're looking at; we do second-stage thinking when we're working out what to do about it.

- *First-stage thinking* asks: 'What are we looking at?'
- *Second-stage thinking* asks: 'What shall we do?'

We do first-stage thinking by recognising something that fits into some pre-existing mental pattern. We can call these mental patterns 'ideas'. Ideas are arrangements of experience in our minds. They allow us to make sense of our experiences; indeed, they are the means by which we have experiences.

The output of first-stage thinking is language. (Or, more correctly, representation: we could draw a picture of it, record it on video or represent it as a piece of music.) We encode experience so that we can manipulate the code at the second stage. We name an object or event; we translate complex activity into an equation; we simplify a structure by drawing a diagram.

In second-stage thinking, we judge what we've perceived in order to achieve some sort of outcome. And we judge by manipulating the language by which we've represented our perception. Having looked at an object and named it as, say, a 'cup', we apply logic, custom and aesthetics to judge its effectiveness as a cup – or its beauty, or its appropriateness to our needs, or whatever. Having labelled a downturn in sales as 'a marketing problem', we use market research, spreadsheets, past experience and critical scrutiny of the marketing department to judge how best to solve it.

We can begin to manage a group's thinking by separating the two stages of thinking. If we're conscious of what stage we're at in our thinking, we can apply the tools and techniques appropriate to that stage.

We're highly skilled in second-stage thinking. We're taught it at school: we learn verbal and mathematical languages, we're encouraged to analyse, to deduce, to argue and to evaluate. (Debate is a form of second-stage thinking.) We're so good at it that we regard it as the sum total of thinking. IQ (intelligence quotient) is a measure of our ability to manipulate language and symbols. So sophisticated is our second-stage thinking that we can construct machines to do the thinking for us (or at least some of it): computers are second-stage thinking devices.

We aren't nearly so skilled at first-stage thinking. We're taught almost no techniques to help us improve our perception. Yet a change in our first-stage thinking can have dramatic consequences at the second stage. If we decide that the cup isn't a cup but a trophy – or a vase, a mug, a chalice – our second-stage thinking about it will change. Our 'marketing problem' may actually be a 'product quality problem', a 'distribution problem', 'a personnel problem', a 'macroeconomic problem' – or a subtle combination of all five.

We tend to ignore first-stage thinking, for a number of reasons. We have plenty of technology to help us perceive more effectively, but few thinking techniques as sophisticated as the second-stage thinking techniques of mathematics or logic. Our work focuses on results, so we accord greater prestige to second-stage thinking than to first-stage thinking. Managers in particular tend to admire decisiveness; they might disparage careful exploration of an issue as 'slow'. More deeply, challenging our perceptions can be uncomfortable; it can create anxiety or even threaten our sense of sanity.

But no amount of good second-stage thinking can make up for faulty or inadequate first-stage thinking. Good thinking pays attention to both stages of the process. And if we want to improve our thinking, developing our first-stage thinking is often a good way to start.

The great Swiss psychologist Carl Jung developed the two stages of thinking into two sets of paired complementary functions: *sensation and intuition* at the first stage; *feeling and reasoning* at the second. Jung himself used this model as the basis of a theory of personality types; it's the basis of the Myers-Briggs type indicator.

Using Jung's model, we can formulate the kind of questions we might ask at each stage of the thinking process. First-stage thinking questions include:

- 'What can we see?' (Sensation)
- 'What might it mean?' (Intuition)

Second-stage questions include:

- 'What can we do?' (Reasoning)
- 'What shall we do?' (Feeling)

These four questions create the foundations for four thinking conversations.

Four thinking conversations

This model suggests four types of conversation that we can use at the different stages of our thinking.

A conversation for relationship

First stage: sensation

Whatever we can accomplish in a meeting is determined by our relationship: what we can say to each other, or ask of each other, is defined by the terms of that relationship; the actions we can commit to are limited by the boundaries of the relationship.

A conversation for relationship is intended to create and generate the relationship necessary to achieve our objectives. It's an exploration. Who are we? How do we relate to the matter in hand? What links us? How do we see things? What do you see that

I can't see? What do I see that you don't see? In what ways do we see things similarly or differently? How can we understand each other? Where do we stand? Can we stand together?

Conversations for relationship are tentative and sometimes awkward: a meeting at a social event or the opening of a job interview are good examples. Serious conversations for relationship go beyond social conversation or finding common interests. In meetings, this first conversation is often rushed or ignored, simply because it can feel embarrassing.

A conversation for possibility

First stage: intuition

First-stage thinking finds its fullest expression in this second conversation. A conversation for possibility is not about whether we can do something. It seeks to find new ways of looking at reality. It's a conversation exploring a wide range of perceptions, making distinctions without judging them, looking for something new.

There are a number of ways of looking at things differently. We could look at something from a different angle, by asking group members for differing interpretations. We could distinguish what we see from our interpretation of it. We can isolate one element of a situation and concentrate on it, or relate elements into a larger web of perceptions. We can create metaphors of an issue in order to see it in a radically new light. Conversations for possibility are potentially a source of creativity: brainstorming is a good example.

A conversation for possibility is necessarily a delicate one. Possibility is, by definition, ambiguous; it may be difficult to articulate. For these reasons, conversations for possibility may collapse into a conflict of perceptions unless they're well managed.

- *Welcome wild ideas*. **People must know that they're allowed to speculate, to utter ambiguous, half-formed or crazy ideas.**

- *Prohibit second-stage thinking.* Don't allow judgements, criticisms or even analysis of ideas. Listen for the words 'right' or 'wrong'. Possibilities are never right or wrong: they are simply possibilities. For every contribution, ask: 'What's interesting about it?' Encourage the group to build on ideas. Say: 'Yes and...' rather than 'No, but...'
- *Decide nothing.* Make it clear that no decisions will be taken until this conversation is over: that people are not committing themselves to anything by contributing.
- *Be on the lookout for 'conversations of no possibility'.* For example, when people remark that 'this is the way it is and always will be.' Listen for statements of fact and challenge them: 'facts' may be merely well-established opinions; they certainly are not possibilities. Challenge, too, statements including words like generally', 'usually', 'certainly', 'always'. They are probably assertions of no possibility. Ask: 'In what circumstances?'
- *Challenge opinions or meanings.* Ask: 'What makes you say that?' 'What leads you to that conclusion?' Ask explicitly for alternative interpretations of observations.
- *Challenge the limits of the group's observation* by asking: 'What if...?' or 'How about...?'
- *Manage the emotional quality of the conversation.* Make it clear that you don't welcome inappropriate jokes, personal judgemental comments or emotional 'explosions'.

A conversation for opportunity

Second stage: thinking

Many of the good ideas we generate in meetings never become reality because we fail to map out clear paths of opportunity. A conversation for opportunity is designed to construct such paths. It's fundamentally a conversation about planning.

Where can we act? What could we do? Which possibilities do we build on? Which are feasible? The bridge from possibility to opportunity is measuring the conditions of satisfaction: targets, milestones, obstacles, measures of success. How will we be able to judge when we have achieved an objective?

We hold a conversation for opportunity to choose what to do. We assess what we would need to make action possible: resources, support and skills. The group's thinking here is more focused than in a conversation for possibility: in choosing from among a number of possibilities, we're finding a sense of common purpose.

Take care not to kill off possibility by translating it into the detailed plans of opportunity. Keep the spirit of the original idea alive by continually asking: 'What are we trying to achieve?'

Conversations for opportunity can become more imaginative and exciting if we place ourselves in a future where we have achieved our objective. What does such a future look like and feel like? What's happening in this imagined future? How can we plan our way towards it? Usually we plan by starting from where we are and extrapolate current actions towards a desired objective. By 'backward planning' from an imagined future, we can find new opportunities for action.

A conversation for action

Second stage: feeling

A conversation for action produces commitment. Translating opportunity into action requires more than agreement: we need to generate a promise, a commitment to action.

This conversation relates to Jung's feeling function. We are asking others to commit with hearts as well as minds. If we take that commitment for granted, we can create anxiety, resentment and pain in others. If we make too many commitments, we can cause ourselves stress.

A conversation for action is a dynamic between requesting and promising.

1. I make a request that you do something by a certain time. I must make it clear to you that this is a request, and not an order. Orders may get immediate results; but they are unlikely to get more than the minimum, and they may not achieve results next time.
2. You have four possible responses to this request:
   – You may accept.
   – You may decline.
   – You may commit to accept or decline later ('I'll let you know by...').
   – You may make a counter-offer ('No, but I can do something else for you...').
3. The conversation based on this request and these responses will result in a promise: 'I will do x for you by time y.'

A meeting will probably contain all four types of conversation: relationship, possibility, opportunity, action. They will only be truly effective if conducted *in order*.

A conversation's success depends on the success of the conversation preceding it. An unresolved conversation will continue within the next conversation, *in code*. Unresolved aspects of a conversation for relationship can be transformed into hidden agendas or festering 'personality clashes'. Possibilities left unexpressed may become missed opportunities. Above all, if the conversation for action in a meeting doesn't result in real commitment, we must ask whether we've left any other conversation unfinished.

These four conversations map well onto Tuckman's four-stage model of group development.

1. A conversation for relationship is appropriate at the forming stage, when a group is new or responsibilities for tasks are unclear.

2. The storming stage is characterised by conflict between people's perceptions, their versions of reality. A conversation for possibility contains the techniques to take the group through this stage so that it emerges trusting, open and secure.

3. In a conversation for opportunity, the group finds the common purpose and values of the norming stage, focusing on results, choosing a course of action and channelling its thinking into planning.

4. Finally, in a conversation for action, the group is truly performing: exchanging requests and promises honestly and freely, expressing commitment and getting things done.

This integrated model gives us a powerful tool for improving a meeting's thinking. Tuckman offers a useful explanation of group development; Jung suggests the different kinds of thinking that are appropriate at each stage. With a set of conversations to help us manage the four stages, we can begin to combine effective thinking with positive group behaviour – and manage our meetings in a more disciplined way.

Making our thinking visible

We saw in Chapter 3 how our conversations benefit from visualising our thinking. We can use our bodies to make our ideas clearer, and we can use a range of technologies to help us. We can resort to models, diagrams, slides or holograms; to interactive whiteboards or a scrap of paper. And we can use 'mental technologies', techniques that make our thinking more vivid and accessible to others. It's how we use the technologies that matters.

Creating a clear focus: six thinking hats

Thinking in a group should seek to do two things:

- *Distinguish ideas from people.* 'Ego thinking' (which
  we explored in Chapter 3) creates a kind of emotional
  investment in an idea by identifying it with the person
  thinking it. Criticise the idea and we can find ourselves
  attacking the person. Making ideas the property of the
  group allows us to process them with less potential for
  conflict.
- *Focus our attention.* The group should be thinking
  together: about the same issue, and in the same way.
  Simply using the same words may not be sufficient: a
  single word can have multiple connotations,
  depending on who's using it. We should all be clearly
  focused on the same area of concern; and we should
  know what kind of thinking we are doing at any
  point.

Edward de Bono's 'six thinking hats' achieve both aims. They're
what de Bono calls 'directed attention thinking tools'. The hats
allow us to separate ideas from people, and they allow us to
focus on one kind of thinking at a time. It would be utterly
inappropriate to suggest that someone is a 'red-hat thinker' or
a 'black-hat thinker'. Anybody can use the hats whenever they
want: they can simply put one on and then take it off. Indeed,
using the hats allows people to make remarks that they might
ordinarily not risk making.

De Bono suggests that we label every contribution to a
conversation by means of a coloured 'hat' that the speaker
is 'wearing' as they make it. Chairs can also ask participants
deliberately to make contributions 'wearing' a particular hat.

Edward de Bono's six thinking hats

- *White hat.* Facts and figures.
- *Red hat.* Emotion, feelings, hunches and intuition.
- *Black hat.* Caution, judgement, fitting propositions to facts.
- *Yellow hat.* Advantages, benefits, savings.
- *Green hat.* Creativity, new ideas, exploration, suggestions.
- *Blue hat.* Thinking about thinking, control of the thinking process, 'points of order'.

We can use the hats informally or systematically. Judging which hat to pick at which point can become a sophisticated chairing skill in itself.

Technologies for thinking

Improving our thinking begins with developing our first-stage thinking. If we can see a problem more clearly, deeply or imaginatively, then our second-stage thinking will have more to work with.

Many techniques and technologies have appeared over the years to help us make our thinking visible in meetings. Yet it's surprising how many meetings continue to hold conversations with no visual element whatever. Participants might use computer-generated slides in a presentation – most of which are as likely as not to display words rather than pictures. Some meeting rooms are equipped with whiteboards – many of which are now interactive – or flipcharts. Lo-tech tools like sticky notes can be hugely effective. The key is to be able to use a range of techniques with these tools to help us visualise our ideas.

Nearly all the visual thinking techniques that have grown

up in recent decades seek to display the *structure* of a problem. To quote David Straker, who runs a highly informative website on thinking techniques: 'The size of the problem is simply determined by the combination of the number of information pieces and the number and type of relationships *between* the pieces.' The structure of a problem depends also on its *type*. Straker himself lists six types: post-up, swap sort, top-down tree, bottom-up tree, information maps and action maps. Dan Roam, in his book *The Back of the Napkin*, develops the idea of structure by suggesting that the six 'Kipling' questions – Why, Who, What, When, Where and How – can all be represented by a core set of visual symbols.

Two technologies in particular have proved enormously successful in making use of our capacity to think visually. Both claim not merely to represent our thinking more effectively, but actually to help us think more creatively. Both are excellent examples of first-stage thinking tools.

Mind maps and rich pictures

Mind maps are diagrams representing words, ideas, tasks or other items, linked to and arranged around a central key word or idea. We can use mind maps to generate, structure and classify ideas, as well as the connections between them. They are regularly promoted as memory aids, and thus as useful study and revision tools.

Mind maps are closely associated with Tony Buzan, who claims to have developed the concept around the year 1970. His book *Use Your Head* introduced the idea to a wide public. He introduced 'iMindMap', a software program, in 2006, although he personally still prefers to draw mind maps freehand.

Buzan explains mind maps as examples of what he calls 'radiant thinking'. Standard linear notes, he suggests, obscure key words, hamper memory, waste time and fail to stimulate creativity. They fail to exploit the brain's natural capacity to think associatively. A mind map radiates from a single image. Every word and image connected to the central image becomes a 'subcentre of associations'. In his own words, a mind map 'represents a multi-dimensional reality, encompassing space, time and colour'.

In *The Mind Map Book*, Buzan suggests four sets of guidelines for creating mind maps:

- *Use emphasis*. **Always use a central image. Draw images throughout the map, using three or more colours. Give your images dimensions, and vary the size of printing, lines and images.**
- *Use association*. **Draw arrows, colours and codes to connect elements within the map.**
- *Be clear*. **Use sheets of paper in 'landscape format' (the long side horizontal). Keep printing as upright as you can. Print key words on lines: only one word per line. Make line length equal to word length. Connect lines to other lines (no 'free-floating' lines.) Make central lines thicker. Make images as clear as possible. Draw boundaries around branch outlines.**
- *Develop a personal style*. **Each mind map you draw should be slightly more imaginative and beautiful than the last.**

Mind maps are increasingly widely used, but they are not without their critics. Part of the reason for their success is the idea's simplicity: mind maps are highly adaptable tools that can usefully improve our thinking about a wide range of problems. Indeed, their very ease of use may be one of the factors contributing to a groundswell of criticism against them. When I introduce mind maps in training sessions, people often say: 'Mind maps? I've tried them; they don't work for me.'

The resistance may be due to the fact that mind maps are often misunderstood. The real benefit of a mind map, as with any visualising tool, is the process of drawing it. It's not the mind map itself that improves the quality of our thinking; it's *drawing* the mind map.

In order to draw a mind map, we have to think actively about the material. We have to choose a main topic and choose material to support it. We have to think about what key words will adequately summarise our ideas, what pictures to draw to illustrate them, and about how everything fits together. The more traditional note-taking techniques we may have learnt at school are little more than copying exercises: they encourage us to gather information, almost literally mindlessly. Mind maps force us to inhabit the information and recreate its structure in our own minds.

Minute-taking offers a powerful example of this benefit. Administrators often take notes in meetings by frantically recording as much of what they can hear as possible. (They may use shorthand to help them do so.) The result can be page after page of poorly transcribed script that is almost impossible to decipher after the meeting. Mindless note-taking results in mindless notes. Results can improve dramatically if we use a mind map. Drawing the map forces us to listen and to make sense of what is happening in the meeting. We must note down *only* the key information that we need; the map doesn't allow us to transcribe what people are saying. When we write up the minutes later, the map once more forces us to make sense of the meeting, rather than simply reproducing people's words. Result: minutes that intelligently record what happened at the meeting.

Using a mind map to record a meeting

- Use plain paper, at least A4 size. One sheet per item, in landscape format (long side horizontal). Put the item number and name in a circle in the middle of the page. You can prepare blanks before the meeting. Have pens of three colours available.
- Note down key ideas as they arise, with initials if appropriate. Add ideas where they logically connect.
- Use different colours for actions and information.

Rich pictures are variants on mind maps that are particularly valuable in picturing a large-scale system like an organisation or network. Rich pictures grew out of Soft Systems Methodology (SSM), developed during the 1960s and 1970s by Peter Checkland and his students at Lancaster University. The aim of SSM was to design IT systems that actually supported the networks of people using them. Checkland's key insight was that problems don't exist separately from the people involved in them; to solve a problem within a human system means understanding the multiple viewpoints of the actors within it.

Rich pictures help us do first-stage thinking about systemic problems. They help us map not only the obvious facts of a situation, but also abstract or emotional factors like the social atmosphere among the actors. A rich picture represents what we know about a messy situation: the issues, the actors, the problems, processes, relationships, conflicts and motivations. Drawing a rich picture helps us to see not only the obvious facts about a situation, but the emotional and social factors underlying it.

How to draw a rich picture

Begin with a large sheet of paper and a lot of differently coloured pens. Draw what you see happening in the situation. Include everything that you perceive to be problematic or significant: emotions and relationships as well as organisational groupings. Use symbols and metaphors.

All rich pictures include three important components:

- 'Structure' refers to aspects of the work context that are slow to change. These might be things such as the organisational hierarchy of a firm, geographic localities, physical equipment, and so on. Most important, it includes all the people who will use or could conceivably be affected by the introduction of the new system.

- 'Process' refers to the transformations that occur in the process of the work. These transformations might be part of a flow of goods, documents or data.
- 'Concerns' capture people's motivations for participating in the situation. Different motivations create different perspectives on the situation. We might capture concerns in 'thought bubbles'; conflict between participants might be represented by a 'crossed swords' symbol; and so on.

Focusing on structure, process and concerns helps prevent the rich picture from becoming overloaded with detail.

Rich pictures are powerful first-stage thinking tools. They can transform our thinking about a complicated organisational situation and illustrate it in ways we can all understand. Their value becomes especially clear when they're drawn by groups, because they illustrate people's differing perceptions and assumptions about a situation. The rich picture shows us the connections, dead ends, contradictions and possibilities we might otherwise have missed. We may find it hard to see other people's points of view, or to accept the conflicts that are hampering our effectiveness. Rich pictures help us to hold the two conversations of first-stage thinking: the conversations for relationship and possibility.

7

Participating well

For most of us, the word 'participation' probably suggests how we speak in meetings. But participating is more than making our point well; it means being actively present in the meeting, helping others to participate and contributing to the quality of the group's thinking. Participation is about finding our own voice, helping others to find theirs, and helping the meeting to achieve its objectives.

Enquiry and advocacy

Peter Senge, author of *The Fifth Discipline*, uses the words 'advocacy' and 'inquiry' to describe participation. Talking is principally the means by which we advocate our point of view, our ideas and our thinking. Listening is the means of enquiring into the other person's point of view, their ideas and their thinking.

The best conversations balance advocacy and inquiry. They are a rich mix of talking and listening, of stating views and asking questions.

Three ways to encourage participation

Let's think first about how to encourage others to participate. The important skills here are the skills of enquiry – the skills of good listening. The skills of enquiry help us to give others the respect and space they deserve to develop their own ideas – to make their thinking visible.

Paying attention

Attention means concentrating on what the other person is saying.

That sounds simple: how can we listen without paying attention? Of course, we do it most of the time. We think we're listening, but we aren't. We finish other people's sentences for them. We interrupt. We moan, sigh, grunt, laugh or cough. We fill pauses with our own thoughts, stories or theories. We look at our watches or around the room. We think about the next meeting, or the next report, or the next meal. We frown, tap our fingers, destroy paperclips and glance at our diaries. We give advice. We talk.

A lot of what you hear when someone is speaking to you is *your effect on them*. If you are paying proper attention, they will become more intelligent and articulate. Poor attention will make them hesitate, stumble and doubt the soundness of their thinking. Poor attention makes people more stupid. And that makes the group less intelligent.

Listening well means helping somebody find their own ideas. The mind containing the problem probably also contains the solution. Their solution is likely to be much better than ours *because it's theirs*.

Our face will show the other person whether we are paying them attention. In particular, our eyes will speak volumes to them about the quality of our listening. We often don't know what our face is doing when we listen. We may think we're listening but some tick or expression is saying to the other person: 'I'm bored' or 'I feel threatened by what you're saying' or 'someone much more interesting has just walked into the room.'

By behaving *as if* you're interested, you can sometimes *become* more interested. Discipline yourself to use an expression that tells the other person you're interested in what they're saying – and that you are not in a rush.

Treating the speaker as an equal

You'll only participate well if you treat others as equals. The moment you make your relationship unequal, the quality of their thinking will suffer. If you place yourself higher than them in status, you will discourage them from thinking well. If you place them higher than you, you will start to allow your own inhibitions to disrupt your attention to what they are saying.

Patronising the speaker is the greatest enemy of equality in conversations. This conversational sin derives from the way we are treated as children – and the way some of us subsequently treat children. It can be subtle: patronising behaviour often covers itself in the guise of being caring or supportive. But it stops people thinking for themselves. It makes them less intelligent. You can't patronise somebody and pay them close attention at the same time.

Cultivating ease

Good thinking happens in a relaxed environment. Cultivating ease will allow the group to enquire more deeply and discover more ideas.

We have become accustomed to urgency. If we aren't working flat out – chased by deadlines and juggling 50 assignments at once – then we think we're not worth our salary. And we sometimes carry this air of urgency with us into meetings. If we aren't in a hurry, we think, the goal can't be worth hurrying for.

We're wrong. Urgency keeps people from thinking well. Sometimes, the best results only appear by relaxing: by paying attention to someone else's ideas with a mind that is alert, comfortable and at ease. When we are at ease, the solution to a problem will sometimes appear as if by magic. The swirl of distractions settles into a clear, comfortable sea of thoughts from which ideas emerge like dolphins coming up for air.

Cultivate ease. Slow down. Focus on what needs to be done; put to one side anything that distracts from the job. It's the quality of the decision that matters, not how quickly you reach it. A poor decision made fast will cause more damage than no decision at all.

Stating your case

The ability to persuade and influence has never been in more demand. The days of simply telling people what to do and expecting them to do it are long gone. Now we must all be able to 'sell our ideas'. The progress of our careers may depend on how well we can speak at meetings. Making our point is our opportunity to make our mark and to contribute positively. It's our chance to be noticed.

Applying some very simple principles will make an immediate difference. Nerves can often take over just at the moment we open our mouths. They may reveal themselves in our shallow breathing, a thin voice, hurried and stuttering words. Here are a few actions that will make a real difference:

- *Set the pace by your speaking*. **If the meeting is rushing, slow down. If the conversation is flagging, inject energy. Take the lead.**
- *Modulate your voice*. **Listen to the music of your voice and try to make it more interesting. Emphasise your points just a little more. Make sure you are speaking loudly enough. Lower the tone of the voice so that you**

don't sound shrill. Breathe deeply so that your voice gains body.

- *Express yourself accurately.* Beware the temptation to generalise to make your case more convincing. Words like 'always', 'never' or 'everybody' will invite others to pick holes in your argument. On the other hand, try not to contradict yourself! Phrases like 'although, of course', 'well, at the same time' and 'on the other hand' may confuse your listeners rather than enlighten them. Be specific. Don't deliver too much evidence at once.
- *Look at the group.* Look, in particular, at their eyes. (Even if they aren't looking at you.) Don't look at your notes, at the table, at the floor or at the ceiling. Don't favour any one person. Include everyone in your gaze.
- *Keep calm.* If necessary, hold something to keep your hands still – but don't fiddle with it.
- *Be fearless.* If you know your point is valid, have the courage to support it. If you are genuinely uncertain, say so clearly.

The key to effective persuasion is having powerful ideas and delivering them well. Ideas are the currency of communication. Information alone will never influence anyone to act. Only ideas have the power to persuade. To persuade, we need to assemble powerful ideas and present them well.

The old word for this skill is *rhetoric*. Since ancient times, the art of rhetoric has taught how to assemble and deliver ideas. Few of us – at least in Europe – now study rhetoric systematically. Yet, with a few simple principles drawn from this ancient body of knowledge, we can radically improve the quality of our persuasion.

Logos, ethos, pathos

Aristotle, in his book on rhetoric, claimed that we can persuade in two ways: through the evidence that we can bring to support our case, and through what he called 'artistic' persuasion, which derives from our own skills as persuaders.

Evidence might consist of documents or witnesses: we might use spreadsheets and expertise as evidence to support a case. 'Artistic' persuasion combines three internal traits in you as the persuader:

- **your character or reputation;**
- **the quality of your logic;**
- **the passion that you bring to your argument.**

Character

Character (or *ethos*) is shorthand for the integrity and authority that you transmit to your audience. Why should your listener believe what you are telling them? What are your qualifications for saying all this? Where is your experience and expertise? How does your reputation stand with them? What value can you add to the argument from your own experience? Your character creates the trust upon which you can build your argument.

Logic

Logic is the grammar of argument. We use logic to link a case that we are arguing to the reasons supporting it. Logic comes in two forms:

- *Deductive logic* **assembles a sequence of propositions (called premises) leading to a conclusion. Most deductive arguments use two premises. The first (or major) premise states a general proposition or principle about a class of things; the second (or minor) premise states that a particular instance is a member of that class. The conclusion then shows that the principle** applies to the instance. A classic example – perhaps *the* classic example – is:

All men are mortal. Socrates is a man. Therefore, Socrates is mortal.

An example from business might be something like:

We want to invest in French software companies with a presence in China.
[General principle about the class of companies we are looking for]
Currently, Company A is the only French software company with a presence in China.
[Premise showing that an instance is a member of that class]
Therefore, we should invest in Company A.
[Conclusion showing that the principle applies to the instance]

The aim of deductive logic is always to make the conclusion inescapable.

- *Inductive logic* presents a summarising idea and supports it with other ideas drawn from observation. A simple example might be:

[We should invest in Company A]

Company A is growing in China.
Company A has an impressive record in innovation.
Company A is well managed.

The conclusion of an inductive argument can never be inescapable; it can only ever be more or less probable.

Passion

Passion (or *pathos*) is the commitment and conviction that you bring to your idea. If you aren't fired up by the idea, you can't expect others to be. To show passion may not be 'the done thing' in your organisation. Yet the great inventors, artists and entrepreneurs are distinguished not merely by their talent, but by the burning conviction that drove them to achieve, often against great odds.

You can't fake passion. If you want to persuade someone of the power of an idea, you must feel that power in your soul. This may not be easy. After all, not every idea is worth a great deal of passion. But if you want to do a good job, if you want to make your contribution, if you care about the future of your organisation, then passion is probably not far away.

What's the big idea?

If you want to persuade someone, you must have a message.

What do you want to say? What's the big idea? You must know what idea you want to promote. A single governing idea is more likely to persuade your listener than a group of ideas, simply because one strong idea is easier to remember. We work in a world of too much information and too few ideas. Without a driving idea, you will never be able to persuade anyone to believe or do anything.

Working out a message

You may have to think about this before the meeting – or even during the meeting. Ask yourself:

- '*What is my objective?*' What do you want to achieve? What would you like to see happen?
- '*Who am I talking to?*' Why are you talking about this objective? What does the group already know? What more do they need to know? What do you want them to do? What kind of ideas will be most likely to convince them?

- **'*What is the most important thing I have to say to them?*'** **If you were only allowed a few seconds – and you may only be allowed a brief time – what would you say to convince them?**

Try to create a single sentence in your head. You can't express an idea without uttering a sentence. Does this sentence express what you want to achieve? Is it in language that the listener will understand easily? Is it simple enough? This is particularly difficult when technical specialists try to persuade more senior managers in meetings. The jargon and detail get in the way of the key message that the persuading manager needs to put across.

Taking the meeting with you

You will need to guide your listeners to the point where they will accept this message. You must 'bring them around to your way of thinking'. This means starting where the listeners are and gently guiding them to where you want them to be. Once you are standing in the same place, there is a much stronger chance that you will all see things the same way. Persuading them will become a great deal easier.

We're only persuaded by ideas that interest us. Your listeners will only be interested in ideas that address some need or question in their mind. You may be able to state that need, or you may have to create a need in their minds.

Here is a simple four-point structure that will help you guide your listeners' thinking. I remember it using the letters SPQR (which you may know as the Latin abbreviation of *Senatus Populusque Romanus* – 'the senate and people of Rome'). Whether you know the Roman connection or not, these letters seem to be a good way of remembering the sequence.

Situation

Briefly tell the listener what they already know. This demonstrates that you are 'on their wavelength': you understand their situation and can appreciate their point of view. Try to state the situation in such a way that the listener expects to hear more.

Think of this as a kind of 'once upon a time...' It's an opener, a scene-setting statement that prepares them for what's to come. Try using phrases like: 'We all know that...', 'I think we all agree that...', or 'This is the situation.'

Problem

Now identify a problem that has arisen within the situation. The listeners may know about the problem; they may not. But they certainly *should* know about it! In other words, the problem should be *their* problem at least as much as yours.

Problems, of course, come in many shapes and sizes. It's important that you identify a problem that the listener will recognise. It must clearly relate to the situation that you have set up: it poses a threat to it or creates a challenge within it.

What's the problem?

Situation	Problem
Stable, agreed	Something's gone wrong
Status quo	Something could go wrong
	Something's changed
	Something could change
	Something new has arisen
	Someone has a different point of view
	We don't know what to do
	There are a number of things we could do

Problems can be positive as well as negative. You may want to alert your listener to an opportunity that has arisen within the situation.

Question

The problem causes the listeners to ask a question (or would do so, if they were aware of it). Once again, the listeners may or may not be asking the question. If they are, you are better placed to be able to answer it. If they are not, you may have to carefully get them to agree that this question is worth asking.

What's the question?

Situation	Problem	Question
Stable, agreed	Something's gone wrong	What do we do?
Status quo	Something could go wrong	How do we stop it?
	Something's changed	How do we adjust?
	Something could change	How do we prepare?
	Something new has arisen	What can we do?
	Someone has a different point of view	Who's right?
	We don't know what to do	What do we do? *Or* How do we choose?
	There are a number of things we could do	Which course do we take?

Response

Your response or answer to that question is your message. In other words, the message should naturally emerge as the logical and powerful answer to the question raised in the listener's mind by the problem.

SPQR is a classic story-telling framework. Management consultants also use the model frequently in the introductions to their proposals. *SPQR* allows you to guide the listeners from where they are to where you want them to be: to prepare them for your message and the ideas that support it.

The trick is to take your listener through the four stages quickly. Many speakers intuitively use this structure but get bogged down in telling the story; their listeners soon start wishing they would get to the point. Don't be tempted to fill out the story with lots of detail. As you use *SPQR*, remember these three key points:

- **SPQR should remind the listeners rather than persuade them. Until you get to the message, you shouldn't include any idea that you would need to prove.**
- **Think of SPQR as a story. Keep it moving. Keep the listeners' interest.**
- **Adapt the stages of the story to the needs of the listeners. Make sure that they agree to the first three stages without difficulty. Make sure that you are addressing their needs, values, priorities. Put everything in their terms.**

Choosing when to speak

Deciding when to speak is almost as important as deciding what to say.

If you speak at the start of the conversation, you may be able to set the tone and the parameters of the discussion. You can take control immediately. Of course, you may then lose it.

In the middle of a conversation, a previous remark may trigger yours or establish the foundation for the point you want to make. Perhaps it contradicts yours, allowing you to make the most of the contrast. Perhaps it was poorly expressed, incomplete, irrelevant or overemotional. This is your chance to bring the conversation back on track and make others feel more comfortable.

The end of the conversation may be the strongest point of all to make your case. By waiting patiently for everyone else to have their say – and perhaps tie themselves in knots – you have more time to prepare your message. Now you can impress the meeting with a flash of clear thinking. This could give you maximum control over the final decision. It is a high-risk strategy – after all, you may be misjudging whether the conversation is actually ending – but it can be highly effective.

Problem-solving in meetings

Management is solving problems. Virtually every managerial meeting will involve problem-solving of some kind. Yet our problem-solving skills are often undeveloped. In particular, teams and other groups who meet to solve problems are rarely trained in the techniques they need.

We saw in Chapter 6 that we can divide thinking into two stages. The ideas and techniques in this chapter are mostly about developing our first-stage thinking: about looking at problems more richly and deeply.

Thinking about problems

Tudor Rickards, in his book *Creativity and Problem-solving at Work*, proposes a set of five problem types:

- *One-right-answer problems.* We tend to assume that a problem – almost by definition – must have a solution. In fact, one-right-answer problems are very rare. They must be closely defined and unchanging over time;

most practical problems at work are poorly defined and change their shape continually.

- *Insight problems*. The answers to insight problems surprise us. We discover them, rather than working them out. The discovery is an 'aha' moment. The solution to an insight problem may be logical with hindsight, but we did not arrive at it logically.
- *Wicked problems*. The solution to a wicked problem cannot be validated until we try it out ('I think this raft will bear our weight: shall we go?'). Many problems are of this kind: solving them may be less difficult than implementing the solution, which requires courage and the ability to anticipate the unexpected.
- *Vicious problems*. Vicious problems generate solutions that pose even greater problems. Solving the problem of high ground rents by relocating on a remote Scottish island may create huge personnel problems.
- *Fuzzy problems*. Fuzzy problems have unclear boundaries, making them difficult to solve analytically. Wicked and vicious problems are usually fuzzy, as are 'people problems' and indeed most everyday problems.

We should distinguish between problem-solving and decision-making. They are closely linked but involve very different kinds of thinking. Deciding is committing to a course of action: choosing from among a number of alternatives and making a rational and emotional commitment to that choice. Solving a problem, in itself, may not lead us to do anything; a decision will always result in action of some kind.

Who owns the problem?

Problems in organisations are unlike the theoretical problems we encounter at school or college, primarily because they are 'owned' by real people. Some problems solve themselves, but most problems without owners tend to remain problems without solutions.

First of all, then: identify the problem owner. They will become the task leader for the problem-solving session. Who is the person most motivated to solve the problem? Do they want to do something about it? Most importantly, are they empowered to act? The problem owner can begin the problem-solving process by presenting the problem to the group. They can explain how it arose, how it affects them and the kind of solution they are seeking. The group can then respond by categorising the problem, applying the techniques appropriate to the kind of problem under consideration, and developing a solution.

Categorising problems

Different kinds of problem will require different approaches. How we choose to tackle a problem depends on how we choose to look at it. We can categorise problems broadly in two ways:

- as *presented* problems and constructed problems;
- by examining the *structures* of problems.

Presented problems
Presented problems happen to us. We aren't responsible for their existence, although we have to solve them. Presented problems prevent us getting where we want to go: they are obstacles in our path. Examples include:

- **the photocopier breaking down;**
- **a competitor's new product invading our market;**
- **being stuck in a traffic jam;**
- **a sudden shift in interest rates.**

The defining feature of a presented problem is a discernible gap between what is and what should be. Presented problems create stress. It's like the pressure between two jammed machine parts that threatens to cause damage. It's unwelcome and unpleasant; it causes fatigue. We can relieve such stress in only two ways: by applying pressure or by separation. We can seek to overcome the problem or avoid it: fight or flight.

Constructed problems

Constructed problems, by contrast, are challenges that we set ourselves. A constructed problem doesn't exist until we create it. There may not be anything specifically wrong; we are interested in *possibilities:* of improvement, change or something different. Examples include:

- **gaining a qualification;**
- **improving our performance;**
- **innovating a new product;**
- **increasing market share;**
- **working out a long-term strategy.**

The defining feature of a constructed problem is the created gap between what is and what could be. Constructed problems create tension. It's like the tension in a taut rubber band, stretched between current reality and our vision of the future. It is potential energy: it's exciting and energising, and provokes movement.

Well-structured and ill-structured problems

We can further categorise problems in terms of their structure: as well-structured or *ill-structured*. We can evaluate a problem's structure in terms of its:

- **initial conditions (where we are);**
- **goal conditions (where we want to be);**
- **operators (the means or methods of moving from initial to goal conditions).**

A well-structured problem (WSP) has clear initial conditions, goal conditions and operators. An ill-structured problem (ISP) is unclear in any or all of these respects.

Completing a jigsaw puzzle is a good example of a WSP. Initial conditions are clear: the pieces are jumbled together in the box. Goal conditions are clear: the finished picture is displayed on the box, and we will know precisely when the solution is complete. Operators are clear: categorise pieces by colour, separate all the straight edges, find the corners, compare pieces against the finished picture, and so on. The problem can become more ill-structured in a number of ways: if pieces are missing (initial conditions unclear); if we have no picture on the box (goal conditions unclear); if there are no straight edges, or if all the pieces are of the same colour (operators unclear).

With these two dimensions – presented/constructed, and well-structured/ill-structured – we can now create four categories of problem.

Type 1: Puzzles (presented; WSP)

These are deviations from the norm. We might call them one-right-answer problems. The archetypal examples are technical: a fault in a machine, an interruption in the power supply, a piece of equipment that won't work properly. The classic problem-solving process – diagnose the cause of the problem, remove the cause, solve the problem – will only work for this type of problem.

Type 2: Headaches (presented; ISP)

These, too, are deviations from the norm; but there's no single or obvious right answer. The problem may have no identifiable cause, or have many causes. Trying to solve a technical problem with no technical expertise is an example of a headache. Much traditional problem-solving spends a lot of time and effort trying to turn Type 2 problems into Type 1 problems. Unfortunately, Type 2 problems often have a habit of reverting to type.

Type 3: Planning problems (constructed; WSP)

These are challenges that we set ourselves. We map them out in terms of *objectives, targets, milestones* and *measures of success*. Examples include working out objectives after an appraisal, setting a budget, giving the team a sales or quality target, or organising a project.

Type 4: Dreams (constructed; ISP)

These are 'fuzzy' problems. The objective is to find something new: a product or service, a new process, a new territory, a new set of goals. 'People problems' are often dreams: how to manage or improve a tricky relationship, for example. We are uncertain of the current situation; we may have no precise idea of where we want to go, or how we will know that the problem has been solved. We may not know that we have succeeded until we've tried something (this would be a 'wicked problem').

Dreams demand open minds. Tackling them takes us into the realms of lateral thinking and brainstorming, where we try to step outside the boundaries of our usual thinking. A task leader in a meeting inviting a creative approach might begin by using statements like:

- **'What I'd really like to do is...'**
- **'If I could break all the rules of reality, I would...'**
- **'This problem is like...'**

The only difference between these four types of problem is our perception of them. We choose to see a problem as being of a certain type. How we go about solving it will depend entirely on that choice. The problem may become another type of problem as we explore it. A puzzle, for example, the more we examine it, may very well become a headache! What seems initially to be a creative problem can become a puzzle or a plan. We can also choose to transform a problem, by deliberately changing its type.

The dynamics of problem-solving

We tend to have few mental disciplines for solving problems. Most of the logical processes we learn at school only work for one-right-answer problems: mathematical problems or scientific experiments (though experiments, of course, can have unexpected outcomes). In meetings, we are constantly encountering problems that are more complicated and more ambiguous than the neat problems we are set in the classroom. All the more reason to find a systematic approach that will help us to tackle them.

Structuring the process

We need to structure the problem-solving process, especially if we are working as a group. Everybody in the group must know what the structure is, what tools and techniques they are expected to use, and what behaviours are allowable or inappropriate at each stage. Whatever the problem, it's useful to keep the thinking structure as simple as possible:

1. Identify the problem.
2. Think about the problem.
3. Develop a solution.

The group must be *directed* through this process. Somebody must keep order, preventing the group from jumping forwards or back between stages, urging them to stay with a technique or try something different, controlling the traffic of ideas and behaviour. Responsibility for this facilitative task best rests with a process director, who should be somebody other than the problem owner – probably the Chair. Other participants in the meeting become resources at the service of the problem owner, led in their thinking by the Chair or process director.

An easy way to envisage this is to imagine the group as an

'ideas consultancy'. The Chair is the lead consultant, and the problem owner is the 'client'. The group should treat the problem owner with the same respect they would give any client: listening carefully to their concerns, tailoring their thinking to the specific issues the client brings to the meeting, checking their ideas with the client at various stages. The group may sometimes need to separate itself physically from the client, particularly in order to generate ideas without the danger of being limited by the client's assumptions or negative responses.

Good problem-solving relies on good first-stage thinking. The greatest danger of problem-solving meetings is that the group will leap to a judgement, ignoring first-stage thinking and plunging headlong into the second stage. Resist the temptation: spend more time on the first stage. This applies in all three steps of the process: evidence, interpretation, action. Do not be afraid to spend more time in first-stage thinking, exploring issues, adding information or reconstructing the problem. Such time will rarely be wasted.

Stage one: identify the problem

If we are working out ways to get from where we are to where we want to be, we need first to investigate where we are *as fully as possible*. We must ask three questions:

- **What is the current situation?**
- **Does a gap exist between this situation and a more desirable one?**
- **Are we certain that we do not already have a satisfactory means of closing the gap?**

Obvious as these questions sound, many problem-solving groups fail to ask them. As a result, they waste a great deal of time trying to solve several different problems at once, or irrelevant problems, or problems that do not exist.

Ask the problem owner to present the problem to the meeting. Listen carefully to what they say and ask questions to improve the group's understanding of the issue. *Avoid suggesting solutions*. Group members will probably begin to think in terms of solutions very quickly: encourage them to note them down privately for consideration later. If somebody does suggest a solution openly, 'park' it on a sheet of flip chart paper and move on.

'How to'

Running a 'how to' session is an excellent way to expand the group's first-stage thinking. A 'how to' session opens up our perceptions on a problem, allowing us to explore it, investigate it and identify the problem that's of most interest to the problem owner.

The first step is to ask the problem owner to cast the problem as a 'how to' statement. For example, 'a piece of machinery breaking down' can become 'how to repair the machinery'. The group can then create new 'how to' statements:

- **how to repair the machinery:**
  - *how to stop the machinery breaking down;*
  - *how to achieve targets without using the machinery;*
  - *how to manage with faulty machinery;*
  - *how to build our machinery maintenance skills.*

It's this *range* of 'how to' statements that is important. They create possibilities by enriching our perception of the problem. So the aim of a 'how to' session is to create as many new 'how to' statements as possible. Quantity matters more than quality at the idea-generation stage. An effective 'how to' session might generate 50 to 100 new statements from a single idea.

If the supply of new 'how to's dries up, we can ask four questions to generate more:

- **'If we could solve this problem, what larger problem would we solve?' Answers will tend to be more strategic 'how to's.**

- 'What do we need to do to solve this problem?' Answers will tend to be more tactical, operational, specific 'how to's.
- 'If we fail to solve this problem, what problems will we need to solve?' Answers will be consequences of failure, or problems tangential to the original one.
- 'If we solve this problem, what new problems do we create?' Answers will also be consequences, but this time the consequences of success. Asking this question takes us into the territory of Tudor Rickards' 'vicious problems'.

The problem owner, faced with an array of 'how to' statements, might then sort them and decide which to pursue. Some problems will look like puzzles and others like plans. Some will be headaches and some will be dreams. The most implausible dreams are those with the greatest creative potential. If you want to pursue a creative approach, pick the most implausible idea and work on it. If the idea also has a 'wow' dimension – if the problem owner feels excited by the idea in some way – so much the better.

Stage two: think about the problem

Having identified the problem, and the category it best fits, we can begin to apply the tools and techniques appropriate to the task.

Puzzles

A puzzle is a presented problem, and the essence of a presented problem is that it is outside us. We take no responsibility for its existence – only for solving it or finding a way of living with it. We act on puzzles; we remain fundamentally unaffected by them.

By choosing to look at the problem as a puzzle, we choose to treat it *objectively*: to analyse it rationally, seeking causes of effects or splitting the problem into parts and tackling each part systematically. In order to deal effectively with a puzzle, we must give it as clear a structure as possible.

We tackle puzzles by using heuristics: put simply, methods of finding things out (the word, from the Greek, is related to 'eureka'). A mathematical formula is an example of a well-structured heuristic. Other heuristics may be less exact, but no less useful. Six broad categories are particularly important:

- *Proximity*. **How close are we to the problem? Can we find our way towards the problem by locating it in context or by solving related problems?**
- *One step at a time*. **Can we break the problem down into parts and solve each part in order?**
- *Means and ends*. **Can we separate our goal from the means of getting there? What is our overall objective? What do we need in order to achieve it?**
- *Modelling*. **Can we make a model of the problem? This would simplify it and allow us to manipulate the model so as to assess possible outcomes.**
- *Analogy*. **What is the problem like? Can we find a concrete example of something similar? What are the similarities? What are the differences?**
- *Abstraction*. **What is the overall, simple shape of the problem? Can we summarise it? Does the summary suggest a simple solution? Could we then apply means and ends analysis to work out how to achieve it?**

Headaches

Headaches, too, are presented problems but, unlike puzzles, we cannot be cool and objective about them. They cause us pain. The pain is a sign that we are no longer outside the problem. We may not have been responsible for it, but we have become involved: it affects other parts of our work, we feel forced to take responsibility for its consequences. This discrepancy between our involvement and our lack of responsibility is what makes it a headache.

We can deal with a headache in two ways: use a pain-killer or remove the stress that causes it. The equivalent in problem-solving to an analgesic is known as the 'quick fix'. It treats the symptoms without tackling the cause of the problem. Repeatedly doing things rather than delegating them is a good example of a quick fix. The quick fix may be attractive because it produces immediate results and can therefore be seen to be 'working'. But because the root cause of the problem remains unsolved, the problem recurs and the quick fix becomes a regular fix. We become dependent and, eventually, addicted.

A more effective approach to a headache is to find a way to remove the stress that causes it. This may involve transforming it into a puzzle, a plan or a creative problem. Perhaps we can make the problem more well structured. Or we can move the headache in another direction. We may choose to turn it into a constructed problem. By transforming our perception of the problem, we take responsibility for it: it becomes a challenge that we can feel comfortable accepting, rather than an obstacle that we cannot move.

Planning problems

A planning problem is a constructed problem. The essence of a constructed problem is that we 'own' it. It's not a matter of 'me acting on the problem', but of 'me being with the problem' or rather, of the problem becoming a part of me.

Athletes training for the Olympics are not acting on the problem of how to win; they are living the challenge of improving their performance. Similarly, when we accept the challenge of a constructed problem, we take responsibility for our own performance and for the outcome, whatever it may be. It's always possible to transform a presented problem into a constructed problem. Such a transformation:

- **gives us responsibility for the problem;**
- **helps to convert stress into tension – into potential energy for change;**

- **transforms an obstacle into an opportunity;**
- **widens our choice of action.**

The simplest way to create a constructed problem is to cast it as a 'how to' statement. For example:

How to install a new system throughout the organisation by the end of the year.

This challenge is a planning problem. It's well-structured in terms of initial conditions and goal conditions. To be thoroughly well-structured, we must clarify our operators: our plan, and the measures of satisfaction by which we can judge our success in completing it.

Planning meetings are among the most common in management. They may be relatively straightforward or horribly complicated – depending on the number of activities to be co-ordinated. Leaping to judgement is as much a risk in solving a planning problem as in any other. It's easy to get lost in the complexity of detail and lose sight of your overall objective. Do not assume that everyone agrees on it or even understands it. First-stage thinking here involves asking:

- **'What are we trying to achieve?'**
- **'How will we know when we have achieved it?'**

Work out your plan backwards from your objective, rather than forwards from where you are.

Dreams

Creative problems are fuzzy constructed problems. The less well-defined a problem is, the more amenable it is to creative treatment. We will probably never find ourselves tackling a problem creatively by accident. We must deliberately choose the creative approach. We would make that choice where:

- **we can find no single identifiable cause;**

- **we cannot remove the cause or causes;**
- **we have too little (or too much) information about the problem.**

These factors characterise a good many of the problems we face in our organisations. Creative thinking is not a desirable extra that we might consider bolting on to our existing managerial skills. It is, increasingly, a critical ability that we must all foster.

Deciding to take a creative approach may not be easy. We are straying into unfamiliar territory; we may find nothing, or something with implications far beyond the original problem. We must weigh up, therefore, the possible consequences of *not* 'going creative' on a problem. Suppose we are missing something of enormous benefit by not exploring? Suppose a competitor finds it and puts us out of business?

At the heart of creative problem-solving is an *excursion*. We are taking a journey away from the original problem, to find something somewhere else that we can bring back as a potentially useful solution. In the words of Joseph Campbell, one of the 20th century's most creative thinkers: 'Creativity consists in going out to find the thing that society hasn't found yet.'

A whole industry has grown up in the past 50 years, devoted to developing and promoting creative thinking techniques. Among the earliest is brainstorming, invented in the 1930s by Alex Osborn, an advertising executive. Brainstorming operates – or should operate – according to four rules, set out in the box below.

Alex Osborn's four rules of brainstorming

- *Criticism is ruled out.* Ideas are to be judged later, not during the session.
- *'Freewheeling' is welcome.* The wilder the idea, the better. It's easier to tame down than to think up.

- *We want more!* The more ideas, the more the likelihood of a good new one.
- *Combine and improve.* As well as contributing ideas, team members should suggest ways of improving, combining or varying others' ideas.

Beyond these simple rules, Osborn emphasises the importance of:

- getting going – not waiting for inspiration to strike;
- focus – on the objective of the session, what we want to achieve;
- attention – of the whole team to one kind of thinking at a time;
- concentration – sticking at it, refusing to give up if no ideas come.

In the decades since Osborn published his ideas in his book *Applied Imagination*, a good deal of research has investigated whether brainstorming does indeed help groups to generate creative ideas. The results have been ambiguous: groups don't seem to be as effective as individuals at generating ideas, though they do seem to be able to evaluate and develop ideas more powerfully.

Brainstorming may benefit from a few simple additional guidelines to Osborn's original four principles:

- *Separate individual from group brainstorming.* Ask people to generate ideas individually to begin the process. Gather them anonymously, to encourage the wilder ideas to surface and counter any politics or inhibitions in the team. Then use group brainstorming to group the ideas, build on them, combine them, vary them, develop them and transform them.

- *Set targets*. The discipline of 'scoring' can produce more ideas and help crazier ideas to surface. A target of between 50 and 100 ideas in 10 minutes is not unreasonable for a competent team of about seven people.
- *Vary the session's structure*. Change the way the session runs by:
- briefing the team with the problem a day beforehand, to allow for private musing and 'sleeping on the problem';
- beginning the session with a warm-up exercise, unrelated to the task in hand;
- taking breaks between techniques, to allow people's minds to relax and discover new ideas.

In the last 50 years, a wide range of creative thinking techniques have been developed. Edward de Bono has contributed a host of ideas, including the principle of lateral thinking. In the 1960s, George Prince and William J J Gordon developed a body of research that became known as Synectics. Prince and Gordon sought out the behaviours that liberated managers' thinking in meetings and codified them into a set of techniques. Gordon emphasised the importance of '"metaphorical process" to make the familiar strange and the strange familiar'. He expressed his central principle as: 'Trust things that are alien, and alienate things that are trusted.' This paradoxical idea encourages new ways of looking at a problem; in effect, developing our powers of first-stage thinking. Later writers like Roger van Oech have developed new techniques and tools of a similar kind, all intended to give us, in van Oech's words, 'a whack on the side of the head'.

Nearly all the creative thinking techniques that have emerged in the last half-century revolve around the idea of associative thinking. If we can make new mental connections between a problem and some other idea or element of reality, we can look at the problem in new ways. Principally, the sources of new connections are of two kinds:

- *Metaphorical techniques* ask us to look at a problem in terms of something else, preferably chosen at random. We might pick a word and look for connections to the original problem. We might ask how a different kind of person might tackle the problem. We might ask how solving the problem is like some other kind of activity, again chosen at random. (We've already discussed the power of metaphor in Chapter 3.)
- *Reversal techniques* suggest that we turn the problem inside out, or upside down, or back-to-front. What would the opposite of this problem be? How would the world look if we tried to do the exact opposite of what we think we are trying to do? Reversal often involves seeking what's known as an intermediate impossible: an idea that contradicts all the known laws of common sense or science. A useful trigger phrase in looking for an intermediate impossible is: 'Let's forget about the rules and being logical for a moment.' The most valuable intermediate impossibles are often those that break taboos; we might deliberately look for ideas that are immoral, illegal or otherwise socially unacceptable.

All of these techniques aim to generate ideas that are stepping stones to solutions, rather than solutions themselves. To use them well, a group needs to understand that they are entering 'possibility space': a place where the normal rules of reality don't apply, and where craziness has no dangerous consequences. We are dreaming, looking for new ideas. Most of the good ideas have already been thought of; to find new ideas, we have to look where we least expect to find them. And we need to nurture new ideas; they are often born drowning. More than any other kind of thinking, creativity demands a very specific discipline of care and attention within a group.

Stage three: develop a solution

Whatever the problem we have tackled, we must evaluate any solution we find and develop it as a feasible proposition in the real world. Once the group has presented its solutions to the problem owner and they have chosen the solution that they find most attractive, they should paraphrase it back to the meeting to demonstrate that they understand it. The group as a whole can then evaluate the solution to identify its strengths and potential weaknesses.

Evaluating the solution

The easiest way to do this is to examine the positive, negative and interesting aspects of our solution, in order. The discipline of attending to each set of features in turn will help us to think about them more objectively.

Looking for what is good about a solution will strengthen it. The positive features of any idea will give it added credibility when it comes to be presented to others (who may be all too ready to criticise or reject it). Looking for its weak features will give us the opportunity to work on them, and develop or eliminate them before they see the light of day. By assessing what's interesting about an idea, we begin to reveal its potential impact, and can begin to think about the challenges of implementing it.

1. Identify *positive* aspects of the idea: whatever makes it attractive. Do not worry if you cannot think of many. Persist: think only about positive features. For each one, ask: 'What further benefits would that bring?' For every benefit, ask: 'How else could we achieve them?' Yet more new ideas may suddenly begin to emerge.
2. Now list the aspects that are *negative* or problematic: weaknesses, shortcomings, risks and dangers. For each one, ask: 'So what is it I need to find?' and try to answer with a 'how to' statement. In this way, a single presented problem can easily turn into six or more potential ways of improving the idea.
3. Finally, list the *interesting* aspects of the idea: implications arising from it, the consequences of implementing it, how it will affect other people, potential by-products or spin-offs.

How/how analysis

To strengthen an idea into a workable proposal, we must identify the steps to implement it. Begin with the solution and ask 'How do we do that?'. Identify a small number of actions. For each of them, ask in turn how they can be achieved. After three or four stages, a number of possible 'chains' of action have been worked out, from broad idea through to specific detail. A 'how/how' diagram allows us to see alternative courses of action clearly, to sift feasible courses of action from implausible ones, and to work out a plan of action.

At the final step in the problem-solving process, we are working out the next steps. What began as a meeting to solve a problem has become a meeting to decide on action.

9

After the meeting

No meeting is ever an end in itself. Meetings form part of an ongoing cycle in the lives of managers and organisations. Meetings result in actions, which provoke change, which itself must be evaluated, calling for new meetings.

Everybody has responsibilities after the meeting. The Chair, administrator and participants all have duties to fulfil. If we fail in our responsibilities after the meeting, all the effort that has gone into making the meeting effective and efficient will have been wasted.

The Chair: following up actions

Meetings are judged by their results. The Chair is responsible for ensuring that the actions agreed during the meeting are completed.

Delegate as many actions as possible. This will:

- **relieve you of some of the burden;**
- **give ownership of actions to participants;**

- **demonstrate trust;**
- **build the team.**

All agreed actions should have a named 'Actioner'. Actioners should feel that they 'own' the action: they should understand why they are doing it and have the authority – and resources – to carry it through. The Chair must ensure that nobody takes on an unrealistic amount of work.

Schedule actions to happen as soon as possible. Prompt action is more likely to be taken by participants fired with enthusiasm by the meeting they have just left.

All actions should be agreed in the knowledge of:

- **the meeting's and individual's authority to act;**
- **the implications for other staff, departments, or organisations;**
- **the probable costs;**
- **the resources available.**

Back up all decisions and actions in writing.

A summary action sheet distributed with or before the full minutes can be useful. Other people or departments affected by the action may need to be contacted by memo or by e-mail.

You'll want to follow up actions at an appropriate time. Don't let follow-up disappear amid all the other fires you have to fight; but take care not to pester, particularly if participants have volunteered.

Don't simply reschedule uncompleted actions. Discuss the reasons for failure: is the delegated person overloaded? Perhaps the action was unrealistic or circumstances suddenly changed.

The Chair has one other main responsibility: overseeing the production of the minutes. This may be a delicate task. You may be tempted to amend the administrator's first draft, perhaps for diplomatic reasons, sometimes for political ones. Minutes that are 'economical with the truth' are unprofessional and unethical. More often the problem falls into a grey area where sensibilities must be tactfully respected while accuracy is maintained.

The administrator: writing the minutes

Few of us want to read lengthy minutes. Their very name suggests something brief ('minute' as in 'tiny'). Minutes are a *brief* summary of events – facts, decisions, agreed actions – not a word-by-word description of all that's said. The term 'verbatim minutes' is a contradiction in terms. Be clear from the outset what the Chair requires from the minutes.

Write up the minutes as soon as possible after the meeting: within 24 hours if you can. They should follow the agenda exactly: with identical numbers and item headings. (Look back at Chapter 4 for details about the contents of agendas.) Lay out the minutes as attractively as possible. Allow a wide left margin and plenty of space between items. Highlight actions to be taken: perhaps using bold type, underlining, by placing them in a column on the right-hand side, or by listing them on a separate sheet.

Constructing a minute

The most effective minutes are carefully planned and laid out. Think of constructing your minutes, rather than simply writing them.

Background
You must put the item in context for readers who were not at the meeting. The item title may do the job: otherwise, indicate briefly how the matter arose.

Discussion
How much to include? There's no need to attribute statements to particular individuals unless they ask you to do so. Include references to:

- recent events;
- dates and place names;
- names of people met or interviewed;
- sums of money;
- legal necessities;
- agreements or contracts;
- policies;
- documentation (reports, correspondence);
- names of departments or other organisations.

Decision

A summary of what has been agreed. There's no need to add lengthy reasons or justification for the decision. Summarise the reasons for the decision as briefly as possible.

Action

What is to be done: by whom, when, and where. Actions to be highlighted.

Yours will be the definitive record of the meeting. The minutes must satisfy everybody who attended, and this may require a certain amount of tact. Concentrate on facts, decisions and actions, and you will be less likely to go wrong.

Allow yourself time to check the minutes before presenting them to the Chair and distributing them.

Participating after the meeting

Do you feel that you 'own' the action you have agreed to take? Do you understand why you are doing the job? Are you empowered to do it? You must have the necessary:

- authority;
- instructions;
- resources;
- budget;

- **staff;**
- **information.**

Show willing:
If you don't, you may get picked on!

Don't take on too much:
You may fail and praise may turn to mockery.

Act promptly:
Don't delay. You may forget vital information. Circumstances may change sooner than you think and make the job even more complicated.

Report back as agreed:
Either directly to the Chair or at the next meeting.

Liaise:
Your actions may well link to those of others who were at the meeting and will probably form the basis for future agenda items.

Finally: do you feel that your contribution is being recognised and appreciated? If not: proclaim your success!

10

Different meetings and how to run them

Most managers find themselves regularly holding meetings of different kinds. This chapter examines five of the most common, and offers you guidance on how to conduct them:

- **team meetings;**
- **negotiations;**
- **mealtime meetings;**
- **electronic meetings;**
- **international meetings.**

Go into any meeting with a clear sense of your *purpose*. What do you want to achieve? How are you going to manage the meeting to achieve that objective? What kind of conversation do you need to hold?

Team meetings

Teams must meet frequently. The danger for any regular meeting is that it can become routine: soon it comes to be regarded more with dread than interest. The solution might be to change the way you run team meetings. A team leader who's willing to delegate functions will lead team meetings that are more active, more interesting and more successful.

- *Construct the agenda prior to the meeting.* Anyone who wants to contribute sends a note or adds it to the list. E-mail is particularly valuable for this.
- *Finalise the agenda at the start of the meeting.* Each participant must justify the inclusion of their item. The meeting decides whether it's worthy of discussion (perhaps another team member can solve the problem outside the meeting: a brief conversation, a memo, a report put in the internal post).
- *Allocate timings to all agenda items.* The whole meeting has a maximum length – decided on by you, the team leader – which it must not exceed. The aim is not to fill the allotted time but to complete the meeting as quickly as possible.
- *The agenda is now complete.* Nothing else is allowed until the next meeting.
- *Each item is 'owned' by the participant who submitted it.* As discussion progresses, they must ask:
  - Is the task or problem clearly understood?
  - Is expertise identified?
  - Is knowledge shared?
  - Are they creating a co-operative climate in the group?
  - Is everyone being heard?
  - Can a decision be reached by consensus – without a vote?
  - Is the Chair's role reduced to a minimum?
- *Rotate the Chair's role.* The Chair for each item becomes the minute-taker for the next item, recording the minutes on a flip chart for all to see.
- *Keep to time rigorously.* Clock-watching is the responsibility of the team as a whole.

- *Summarise all decisions and actions at the end of the meeting*. Invite any initial suggestions for the next meeting.

Most team meetings will cover the 'Four Ps':

- *Progress*. Our achievements. Include individual achievements if appropriate. Reflect back to the team what we have done so far to reach our goals. Start with progress because it helps to create a positive feeling in the team.
- *Policy*. How developments elsewhere in the organisation are affecting what we are doing.
- *People*. Any relevant matters affecting team members that will strengthen the team.
- *Points for action*. What we need to do in the future. Any new targets, or special points for action.

This procedure increases the team's ownership of the meeting. A climate of openness allows people to express a range of views, so that the team can arrive at solutions by agreement rather than imposition. In one company where team leaders introduced the procedure, teams cut meeting time by a third.

Team briefing

Team briefing develops the team meeting into a management information system. The objective of team briefing is to ensure that every employee knows and understands what they and others in the organisation are doing – and why. Team leaders and their teams get together regularly, for about half an hour, to talk about issues relevant to them and their work. The team leader's brief is based on a 'core brief' supplied by senior management, but, along with this 'cascade' element of information relayed down the line, all team leaders write their own brief.

The advocates of team briefing emphasise that it also allows teams to evaluate the brief, assess its relevance to their own work, and communicate in turn back up the line. There are a number of other benefits to team briefing:

- *It reinforces management.* The briefing meeting is an opportunity for the team leader to lead. This is particularly important for first-line managers, reminding them of their leadership responsibilities and of their accountability for their team's performance. Team briefing gives management credibility, and ensures that the team hears management information from a manager.
- *It increases commitment.* Briefing improves the team's commitment to their objectives and to those of the organisation. Explaining why a job needs doing is as important as telling people that it has to be done.
- *It prevents misunderstandings.* The 'grapevine' of rumour and speculation is often a threat to team morale and effectiveness. Team briefing helps to keep the vine well pruned!
- *It helps to facilitate change.* To quote Peter Senge: people do not resist change; they resist being changed. Team briefing helps to keep people in touch with what is happening, and to give them the means to contribute to change rather than be victims of it.
- *It improves upward communication.* Asking people for ideas in an information vacuum is like asking them to think without brain cells. People will probably not volunteer ideas if they aren't asked for them; briefing gives senior management the regular opportunity to make that request. It also provides a permanent channel for feedback and other upward communication.

Team briefing, unlike more informal team meetings, must be led by team leaders. Because the briefer should be the manager accountable for the team's performance, it may make more sense to brief people in teams rather than according to managerial status: line managers with their production line teams, for example, rather than with other managers. The choice of briefer can be affected, too, by the size of teams: if teams are too small or too large, communication, control and interaction all suffer.

There's a danger that team briefing can become merely a system of 'top-down' information flow, conducted in a paternalistic, quasi-military manner. It can be easy for senior management to assume that teams only need to know about decisions to commit to them. The success of team briefing depends on fostering genuine dialogue.

Team briefing also relies on systematic implementation to be thoroughly effective. If you are a team leader, you can set briefings yourself; but they will be much more effective if they are part of a wider communication process and structure within your organisation.

Negotiations

Every manager has to be able to negotiate. Doing deals is a fundamental way to achieve goals, but it is a means, not an end. A successful negotiation closes with everybody satisfied; the effective negotiator is delighted when the meeting creates genuine agreement.

The great risk in negotiating is adversarial thinking. The very concept of negotiation implies two sides (or more). As a result, scoring over the opposition becomes the primary strategy. Each side tries to 'get the edge' on the assumption that the other is doing the same. The negotiation becomes a complicated exercise in playing games: secrecy, bullying, hoodwinking – all the familiar symptoms of 'looking out for number one'.

This tacit agreement that negotiation is hostile creates stress, wastes time and generates flawed agreements. As long as this attitude stalks the negotiation, new problems will arise, commitment will suffer, promises will be broken, relationships will deteriorate, and reputations will be bruised.

If you are negotiating, your responsibility is to seek agreement: a specific plan of action to which all parties can commit themselves. You will only achieve real commitment on both sides if you pay close attention to the group's social objectives, moving carefully through the four stages of group development.

Stage one: forming

Relationships at the beginning of a negotiation may, of course, be hostile. The negotiation may be happening against a background of confrontation; people may feel that mutual trust risks being damaged. Whatever the background, people will be expecting hostility because that is our usual experience of negotiation. If you want to break through this hostility to real agreement, you must work hard to establish rapport at the very beginning of the meeting. Rapport is not merely a matter of being polite. Hard questions need to be asked:

- **Do we want to negotiate?**
- **What exactly are we negotiating about?**
- **What are the long-term and short-term objectives, on both sides?**

Know exactly what you want. Where's your bottom line? Beware greed or comparison with others: establish what you need, what you can do without, what will make you truly satisfied.

Ask the same questions of the other side. Imagine yourself in their position. What do they want? What do they *really* want? What are their hopes and plans? Who do they represent? What are they looking for now? How important is it to them? Can you see any way of giving them what they want without losing what you want?

Do your homework: numbers, public and private statements, reports, relationships with background interests. Do not be fooled by initial postures, which may be deceptive. Inspect the

other side's position and *invite them to inspect your own position.*
Admit uncertainty. Expose potential problems on your side.
Honesty will boost your credibility and can be surprisingly
disarming.

Stage two: storming

Establish the areas of difference and examine the reasons for
them. At this stage, what may seem to be differences of objective
may be different versions or perceptions of reality.

Work hard to establish norms: of the task (hard data both
sides can agree on, measures of satisfaction – how will we know
when we have reached agreement?), and of behaviour (what
we find acceptable, what we cannot allow). Demonstrate your
honesty.

Be assertive: neither aggressive in defence of your own
position nor submissive to every proposition from the other side.
Show the other side that you recognise the rules by which you are
both playing: question them, if necessary.

Stage three: norming

Work from agreed norms towards possible solutions or ways
forward. Persist and be patient. Expect the conversation to move
one step forward and two back – or even sideways. Sideways
moves may be clues to new solutions that neither side has
thought of yet.

Be on the lookout continually for new ways to look at the
issue and new ways of handling it. Offer choices and keep options
open. Challenge your own assumptions and resist the temptation
to reject ideas. Work through 'what if' scenarios and invite the
other side to inspect your own thinking. This will only work well
if you are truly open to inspection and willing to alter your views.

Identify sticking points. Are they fundamental differences,
the results of different perspectives or behavioural posturing

(face-saving, demonstrating firmness to vested interests)? When you get truly stuck, go back to first principles. Why are we here? What is our objective?

Stage four: performing

Recognise when you've done the deal. Negotiations sometimes collapse because the negotiators do not notice that they have actually reached agreement. The adversarial nature of negotiation creates the underlying assumption that agreement isn't possible. You may continue to press for advantage after seeming to have won. This is another certain route to breakdown.

Act as if the other side will be your public relations agency. The truth is that they will. What others say about you is how they see you. Your reputation as a negotiator is your most valuable asset in future negotiations. Guard it well.

Mealtime meetings

Business lunches, and now breakfast meetings, are increasingly popular. My own feeling is that they are of limited value. Eating and meeting simply don't mix very well. The informality of a meal can work against the clarity of thinking necessary in a meeting. Objectives may be unclear because there's no formal agenda. The professional and social aspects of meeting are dangerously mixed. Hidden agendas may be hard at work.

The best advice is probably not to schedule mealtime meetings at all. Separate the two activities – and meet before eating! If you find yourself invited to a mealtime meeting, take a few simple precautions:

- **Decide on your own private agenda. Are you going to meet – or eat?**
- **If the meeting is worth attending, you must be prepared not to eat too much.**

- Avoid alcohol.
- Taking notes will be difficult. Arm yourself with a narrow pad that can slip easily between plates and glasses.

Electronic meetings

More and more meetings are happening electronically. Whether as teleconferences over the telephone or as videoconferences, meetings are increasingly events mediated by technology. The development isn't universally welcomed; some sectors seem to be slower at embracing the potential than others. Eric Galvin, a non-executive director for a range of public sector organisations, including the Derbyshire Probation Trust, sees little advance in the UK public sector. 'There remains considerable reluctance to use some of the new technologies,' he says, 'and in my experience enthusiasm for them is often driven by non-executives. Neither teleconferencing nor videoconferencing are high on IT purchasing or commissioning lists.'

The environmental benefits of remote meetings speak loudly in some quarters. 'In one organisation where I work,' says Galvin, 'our very public commitment to "green" policies is making a difference.' The relatively low cost of meeting in cyberspace, compared with multiple flight charges or hotel bills, can also sway the decision to use technology.

For years, the most hi-tech solution was using the phone. Conference calling is still extremely common, although the lack of a visual element has always proved problematic. Tim Fearon, owner of The Extraordinary Coaching Company, explains that 'we are far more dependent on auditory acuity to pick up the nuances of reaction. Meeting on the phone really brings to the fore our ability to build rapport through the use of tonality, pace, linguistic matching, and so on.'

Tim's thoughts provoke some clear, simple guidelines for conference calling:

- *Allow pauses between speakers.* A single word overlapping another speaker will cause considerable delay while the last remark is repeated. A teleconference has its own, peculiar rhythm, which is easily picked up with a little practice.
- *Use names frequently.* Announce yourself by name: particularly if you haven't spoken for some time. Announce whom you are addressing, and who you would like to speak next.
- *Choose your words with care.* The fact that people are not physically together places great weight on the words used. There's a lot of opportunity for misunderstanding and much may need to be laboriously explained in the absence of a visual component.
- *Avoid hidden agendas.* Teleconferences without video are vulnerable to conspiracies: notes passed silently between participants at one end; gestures and facial expressions mocking the ignorance of those at the other end of the line. It's extraordinary how easily such silent behaviour can be picked up at the other end of a phone line. Order must be maintained. On the other hand, it can sometimes be easier to be brutally frank when the other person is 500 miles away.

Videoconferencing has undoubtedly revolutionised the remote meeting. 'Conference calling was never effective for us,' says Simon Meijlink. 'However, Skype video conferencing does work. When you see a face it simply makes the connection better.'

Research seems to bear out Simon's view. Duncan Smith of Mindlab International in Sussex has recently led a project (commissioned by Cisco, a provider of online meeting tools) investigating the effectiveness of different technologies in the workplace. Videoconferencing scored particularly highly in helping groups collaborate. 'When you can see the person you are talking to,' says Smith, 'you get less stressed and you pay more attention. When we use communication technologies that are not visual, we wander. We look out of the window, we check our e-mails, we doodle on a pad. Videoconferencing scores because it encourages us to pay the kind of attention we would pay to a real encounter. It's as close to a face-to-face conversation as we can get using technology.'

The latest stage in the development of videoconferencing is 'telepresence'. For a cool $300,000 (or $300 an hour to rent), you can install a telepresence suite, which creates the illusion that separate video conferencing booths, located anywhere on the globe, are actually part of the same room. Remote participants are shown life-size on HD screens; audio is high-fidelity; room lighting and furnishings are carefully matched to enhance the effect that everyone is together in the same space. Some companies are now offering computer applications to allow participants to log in from their PC or smartphone.

The greatest danger in videoconferencing is that you will assume the meeting is exactly like any other meeting. People may intuitively feel that the technology allows them to leave less time to travel to their point of entry, or to prepare. During the meeting itself, microphones and cameras may pick up distractions that are far more intrusive over a video link than they would be in a room. Silent participants are more obvious on screen, and dominant speakers more dominating.

If you want to make the most of a videoconference, here are some tips:

- *Take time to set up.* **Remind presenters what time the meeting will begin (and check that you've figured in the correct time in different time zones). Review the agenda and ensure that all participants have seen it well in advance. Check connectivity: every participant should have received the call-in numbers and access codes well in advance. At least 10 minutes before the meeting, have them test these and any other connections they'll need to use during the presentation. Ensure that participants have a way to contact you offline: a mobile phone number or an e-mail address. Check out the recording equipment: cameras, microphones, software. Some** online meeting software requires that users pre-load the software. Be sure to start all these processes at least 30 minutes before the scheduled start time to avoid technology-related delays.

- *Prepare.* Every participant should take at least five minutes before the meeting to review the agenda, prepare their contribution and deliver any supporting material.
- *Show up on time.* Punctuality for an online meeting is as important as it is for in-person meetings. It's a disservice to everyone involved – especially to those who did show up on time – if the meeting has to restart or stall to accommodate a latecomer.
- *Manage your physical space.* Remove background distractions: noises, movement, background visual elements that may distract. Look out also for noises you might not normally think about: breathing into the microphone, shuffling papers, tapping a pen on the desk. And think about how you look.
- *Exercise your chairing skills more explicitly than normal.* As with any other meeting, the best Chair manages the air space. In a videoconference, we're all more aware of that space than normal. However sophisticated the technology, you will still need to work to overcome the sense of distance separating members of the group.
- *Be an active participant.* You are on screen, where other participants will be noticing more than they would sitting in a room with you. All of the elements of active participation we covered in Chapter 7 doubly apply during a videoconference.

As we saw in Chapter 1, web technologies are proliferating, converging and morphing. Web conferencing combines videoconferencing with the ability to share documents instantly (Skype offers this facility). Some workgroups are now using collaborative software, based in part on instant messaging.

Virtual meetings are sometimes turning into huddles of shared documents or text. Mindlab International's research strongly suggests that the effectiveness of new technologies depends on the kind of work the group is doing. Looking at three types of business tasks (broadly separated into categories involving visual data, factual and numerical information, and group collaboration), the researchers considered how well different technologies scored on accuracy, efficiency and user experience. This is what they found:

- *Instant messaging* is a good tool for conveying simple segments of numerical data but should be avoided for group-based communications.
- *Telephone conferencing* performed well on data-based tasks for accuracy and user experience, but was low on efficiency.
- *Videoconferencing* scored high on user experience across all three categories, performing well for visual communication and group collaboration, but scored lower on accuracy and efficiency of data communications, as a text interface wasn't present.
- *Web conferencing* performed well in conveying data and for group collaboration across accuracy, efficiency and user experience because it allows participants to share and edit documents in real time, but videoconferencing was better suited to conveying visual data.

As with other technologies and thinking techniques, the key to success is understanding how the group is thinking and what tools are best for the job.

International meetings

We conduct more and more of our business internationally. As organisations operate more globally, and as our own society grows more and more diverse, we find ourselves increasingly meeting with people from different cultures.

How can we begin to make sense of this array of cultures? Fons Trompenaars, a Dutch author and consultant, has identified seven dimensions that describe cultural differences. Trompenaars suggests that different cultures use these dimensions to solve problems in three main areas:

- **problems about our relationships with other people;**
- **perceptions of the passage of time;**
- **problems relating to our environment.**

Five dimensions relate to the ways we deal with each other:

- *Universalism vs particularism.* **What is more important, rules or relationships?**
- *Individualism vs collectivism.* **Do we function in a group or as individuals?**
- *Neutral vs emotional.* **Do we display our emotions?**
- *Specific vs diffuse.* **Is responsibility specifically assigned or diffusely accepted?**
- *Achievement vs ascription.* **Do we have to prove ourselves to receive status or is it given to us?**

In addition, there is a difference in the way societies look at time:

- *Sequential vs synchronic.* **Do we do things one at a time or several things at once?**

The last important difference is the attitude of the culture to its environment:

- *Internal vs external control.* **Do we control our environment or are we controlled by it?**

Three dimensions probably affect international meetings more than any other.

Universalism vs particularism

The universalist, or rule-based, approach is roughly: 'What is good and right can be defined and always applies.' Take the case of trying to cross the street at the red light. In a very rule-based society like the United States, this will still be frowned at even if there is no traffic. In rule-based societies, equality means that all persons, or citizens, falling under the rule should be treated the same.

In particularist societies, the focus is on individual relationships, and on the exceptional nature of circumstances. Again, take the case of trying to cross the street at a red light. In a particularist society, people may think it is no problem if their brothers or friends violate the traffic rule. These people are not 'citizens', but their 'friends' or 'brothers'.

Universalist

- Focus is more on rules than relationships.
- Legal contracts are readily drawn up.
- A trustworthy person is the one who honours their word or contract.
- There's only one truth or reality, which has been agreed to.
- A deal is a deal.

Particularist

- Focus is more on relationships than on rules.
- Legal contracts are readily modified.
- A trustworthy person is the one who honours changes in values or objectives if mutually agreed.
- There are several perspectives on reality relative to each participant.
- Relationships evolve.

If you are meeting in a universalist culture, you may have to use more reasoned argument or codes of professionalism. You may have to accept that what strikes you as rather impersonal and rude is merely part of the way business is done.

If you are meeting in a particularist culture, you may need to engage in more 'small talk', revealing more about your family or personal interests than might seem comfortable. You may also need to take more time before getting down to business.

Achievement vs ascription

This dimension relates to status and leadership. Achievement means that people are judged on what they have accomplished and on their record. Ascription means that status is attributed to you by things like birth, kinship, gender, age, interpersonal connections or educational record. Achieved status refers to doing; ascribed status refers to being.

Achievement-oriented

- Titles are used only when relevant to the competence brought to a specific task.
- Respect for people superior in hierarchy is based on how effectively they do their job and how adequate their knowledge is.
- Most senior managers are of varying age and gender and have shown proficiency in specific jobs.

Ascription-oriented

- There is extensive use of titles, especially when these clarify your status in the organisation.
- Respect for those superior in hierarchy is seen as a measure of your commitment to the organisation and its mission.
- Most senior managers are male, middle-aged and qualified by their background.

The key to success in this dimension is to respect how people see themselves. Praise and explicit reference to the values of the person you are meeting will show that you understand what matters to them.

When you are meeting achievers, respect their knowledge and successes, even if you suspect that they may be over-selling themselves. Refer to your own competence and experience, rather than your job title or position. Do what you can to help the achiever to do better, or to do more.

When you are meeting ascriptives, respect their status, even if you suspect that they lack knowledge or experience. Do nothing to belittle them or lower their status. Refer to yourself in terms of your own position or title.

Sequential vs synchronic

Every culture has developed its own response to time. The time dimension has two aspects: the way a culture structures time; and the relative importance a culture gives to the past, present and future.

Humans structure time in two ways. In *sequentialism*, time moves forward in a straight line, second by second, minute by minute, hour by hour. In *synchronism*, time moves round in cycles: of minutes, hours, days, years.

People structuring time *sequentially* tend to do one thing at a time. They view time as a narrow line of distinct, consecutive segments. Sequential people view time as tangible and divisible. They strongly prefer planning and keeping to plans once they have been made. Time commitments are taken seriously. Staying on schedule is a must.

People structuring time *synchronically* usually do several things at a time. To them, time is a wide ribbon, allowing many things to take place simultaneously. Time is flexible and intangible. Time commitments are desirable rather than absolute. Plans are easily changed. Synchronic people especially value the satisfactory completion of interactions with others. Promptness depends on the type of relationship.

A culture's attitude to historical time affects how individuals behave at any moment. A *past-oriented culture* sees the future as a repetition of past experiences. Respect for ancestors and collective historical experiences are characteristic. A *present-oriented culture* attaches little value to common past experiences or to future prospects. Day-by-day experiences tend to direct people's lives. In a *future-oriented culture*, most human activities are directed towards future prospects. Generally, the past is not considered to be vitally significant to a future state of affairs. Planning constitutes a major activity.

Meeting across cultural barriers

Cultural variation is complicated. The culture of an organisation can differ from that of its host society; an individual's cultural background may differ from that of the organisation they work for. Reading the variations can be intriguing, surprising and, at times, exhausting.

Every meeting is an opportunity to create common ground among those who attend it. The objectives should be realistic and work oriented, but a meeting is also a chance for us to increase our mutual understanding. The best way to minimise culture clash is to make sure that the purpose of the meeting is made clear, and that procedures within the meeting accommodate everybody's expectations.

The meeting will undoubtedly be held in one language. Anybody not fluent in that language will feel seriously disadvantaged. The choice of language for the meeting can itself be a serious cultural, or even political, matter. Arrange for papers to be translated if necessary. You may decide that speakers can speak in any language comprehensible to all, or that they should bring personal translators with them.

Different business cultures create different expectations of meetings. For some, the most important work is conducted outside the meeting: at dinner the night before, or in the coffee break. Your procedures may need to allow for this, by scheduling social events before or after the meeting. Distribute papers well in advance with specific requests for comments. This will give you some idea of the nature of participants' preparation.

Getting agreement on decisions or actions can be tricky in cross-cultural meetings. Are people agreeing to act, or being polite? What is being agreed to? Does each side fully intend to act as its members say they will? Make sure that decisions are specific and understood. In a matter as crucial as a contract, you may even want to take legal advice.

Perhaps the greatest danger in meeting across cultural boundaries is that we find ourselves reinforcing stereotypes. John Mole, in his entertaining book *Mind Your Manners*, says:

> Whether or not they exist in reality, stereotypes certainly exist in the perception of outsiders. And it is in perceptions of behaviour that misunderstandings occur. Avoiding them will make collaboration not necessarily more harmonious but at least more productive.

Mole's book has a wise title. The best way to manage cultural diversity – wherever we come from – is to cultivate good manners.

11

Where to go from here

Meetings are a subject of continual study, comment and downright speculation. In this Chapter, I bring together references to the books, websites, research projects and other resources that I've mentioned in this book. My blog also explores issues and events relating to the material here. You can find it at: http://justwriteonline.typepad.com/distributed_intelligence/.

Introduction

The survey by Microsoft is documented here: http://www.microsoft.com/presspass/press/2005/mar05/03–15threeproductivedayspr.mspx.

Steven G Rogelberg has produced an article about his project, which is available at: http://sloanreview.mit.edu/the-magazine/articles/2007/winter/48207/the-science-and-fiction-of-meetings/.

Chapter 1: What is a meeting?

The recent survey suggesting that 11 million meetings are

held in the United States each day is here: https://e-meetings. verizonbusiness.com/global/en/meetingsinamerica/ uswhitepaper.php.

The other statistics in this chapter are taken from the Rogelberg article cited above.

Chapter 2: How groups work

Tuckman's work on groups is well known and well documented. A good introduction is at: http://www.garfield.library.upenn.edu/ classics1984/A1984TD25600001.pdf.

French and Bertram present their ideas on power in 'The bases of social power', in D Cartwright (ed), *Studies in Social Power* (1959, University of Michigan Press, Ann Arbor).

For Meredith Belbin, go straight to his website: http://www. belbin.com/.

Chapter 3: Conversation: the heart of the meeting

Max Atkinson's book *Lend Me Your Ears* (2004, Vermilion Books, London) is excellent on presentations, and has a lot to say about conversation, principally in Chapter 1.

British Telecom runs an excellent site on conversation skills: http://www.numberoneskill.com/number1skill/dialogics/no1.html.

William Isaac's *Dialogue and the Art of Thinking Together* (1999, Currency books, New York) is at the leading edge of studies into conversation.

For Edward de Bono, go to his own website – http://www. edwdebono.com/index.html – where you'll find details of all his many books.

Nancy Kline's *Time to Think* (1999, Ward Lock, London) is a fascinating study of deep listening.

Chris Argyris's Ladder of Inference is best found in *The Fifth Discipline Fieldbook*, edited by Peter Senge and others (1994, Nicholas Brealey, London).